CW00802771

BOOKS BY PAUL YOUNG

'The End of a Nation'
(Studies in Obadiah)

'The Friend and Promise of God'
(Abraham & Isaac)

'Understanding the Bible'
(Inspiration, Inerrancy & Interpretation)

'Outreach Through the Local Church'
(Problems & Needs)

'Understanding the New Age'
(A detailed look at this movement)

'Raging Waves'
(Studies in Jude)

'Cunningly Devised Fables'
(a look at 13 cults and religions and an overview of their characteristics)

'The Diary of a Prophet'
(studies in Haggai)

'A Glimmer of Light'
(Studies in Lamentations)

'Poisoned Soul'
(The deadly effects of bitterness)

'To be like Jesus'
(Studies in the Fruit of the Spirit)

'Faith Alone'
(Studies in Hebrews 11)

Available from: 31, Fairmeadows, Maesteg, UK, CF34 9JL.

Preachers, Poets, Saints and Singers

31 days with
Christians from Wales

PAUL YOUNG

authorHOUSE®

AuthorHouse™ UK
1663 Liberty Drive
Bloomington, IN 47403 USA
www.authorhouse.co.uk
Phone: 0800 047 8203 (Domestic TFN)
       +44 1908 723714 (International)

Published by AuthorHouse 04/14/2020

ISBN: 978-1-7283-5234-3 (sc)
ISBN: 978-1-7283-5233-6 (e)

Print information available on the last page.

Scripture quotations marked NIV are taken from the Holy Bible, New
International Version®. NIV®. Copyright © 1973, 1978, 1984 by International
Bible Society. Used by permission of Zondervan. All rights reserved. [Biblica]

Scripture quotations marked KJV are from the Holy Bible, King James Version
(Authorized Version). First published in 1611. Quoted from the KJV Classic
Reference Bible, Copyright © 1983 by The Zondervan Corporation.

Scripture quotations marked NKJV are taken from the New King James Version.
Copyright © 1982 by Thomas Nelson, Inc. Used by permission. All rights reserved.

This book is printed on acid-free paper.

INTRODUCTION

Wales is a small country attached to England along its eastern border and facing the Irish Sea towards the west. It has been said that its only use is to separate the English from the Irish! The population today is just over three million people and it has devolved political powers exercised by the Welsh Government from the Assembly in Cardiff. The people today all speak the common language of English, but about 18% are also fluent in Welsh and this may increase as there is significant emphasis upon pursuing the Welsh language with a growing number of Welsh medium schools. Sadly many Christian places of worship have closed as society has become increasingly secular, with some of the old industrial valleys having the highest percentages, in Britain, of people with no religious affiliation.

Historically Wales was largely subdued by the Romans who exercised control from their centres in the four corners of the Principality: Caerleon, Carmarthen, Caernarvon and Chester. Gradually Christianity was introduced and the church in Wales flourished and for a number of centuries was independent of Canterbury with its own history and practices as the Celtic Church. In the Middle Ages there was a great deal of military conflict as the English crown subdued Wales and incorporated it into the nation of Britain, especially after the Norman Conquest. Henry VII who founded the Tudor dynasty was Welsh and he helped bring about the eventual union of the two nations, though the Act of Union was passed during the reign of his son, Henry VIII, in 1536.

Religiously Wales has seen many revivals, some affected the whole nation, while others were in particular localities only. The result is seen in the huge number of Nonconformist chapels which have been erected, some of them seating 1,000 people and more. This particularly developed during the industrialisation of the nation as Wales became the first industrialised nation on earth, which meant that more people were engaged in industry than worked the land. In the nineteenth century the iron capital of the world was Merthyr Tydfil and it was there that world prices for iron were set. Swansea developed as a copper smelting centre, while Llanelli set world prices for tinplate and Cardiff for coal. During the late seventeenth century through to the mid twentieth century the nation was vibrant with heavy industry such as the production of iron, steel & copper and the mining for coal and also slate in North Wales. This led to huge influxes of migrant workers, especially from parts of England and Ireland. The former agricultural society was transformed into valleys with furnaces, mines, terraced housing and places of worship.

Along with industrialisation came the need for housing and new towns sprang up and settlements were established. Also railways and canals were constructed for the transporting of goods to the coast for export through the ports of Newport, Cardiff, Barry, Porthcawl, Swansea and Llanelli. These became thriving centres of population and eventually outgrew the inland settlements which today are very much in decline due to the closure of industry. Into this mixture of thriving industries came the need for political organisation and the struggle between owners and workers was a continuing one. The first Labour MP, Keir Hardie, was elected for Merthyr Tydfil and eventually the Labour Party and the trade union movement became strong. The socialist Labour party enjoyed and still enjoys the support of the old industrial communities of the South Wales valleys even though the industries have long gone. The only Welsh Prime Minister was Lloyd George a Welsh speaking Liberal from North Wales in the early twentieth century. However, James Callaghan was Prime Minister in the 1970s and though living in England represented the Welsh constituency, 'Cardiff South East'.

The communities in the days of industrialisation were vibrant with debate, evening classes and the desire to learn but also a realisation of the spiritual. Great preachers were born into those communities. They were people who knew God and lived lives of integrity. They could hold congregations with their powerful oratory but also instilled Biblical truth because they lived and breathed the message of the Gospel. They spoke out against the evils of society and drew people into a living relationship with God. The nation had also been visited by great preachers of the Methodist Revival such as John Wesley and George Whitefield. In modern times Billy Graham and Luis Palau have conducted evangelistic meetings in Wales. The spiritual, Biblical and Christian heritage of Wales has been great but it is rapidly being lost and it is said that less than 5% of the population regularly attend church. The need of the hour is for Christians to be true to their faith, to demonstrate the reality of their commitment to Christ by living righteous lives, while the regularity of church attendance must be addressed and prayer both corporate and personal needs to be engaged with real fervour. Also evidential preaching needs to be taken seriously both publicly in the pulpit and personally by each Christian. God's glory may have departed from Wales but there are still enough true Christian believers to reverse the trends by making the sacrifices needed and with God's help revival may sweep our nation again. That must be our prayer.

The impetus for this very short book was hearing that someone was doing something similar for French Christians from the past. It caused me to wonder whether it would be worth doing some delving into history as far as Wales was concerned. So I simply noted very quickly a list of Christians from bygone days about whom I had read and decided to write a brief biography on each one. The discipline I imposed was that each account would only cover two sides of an A4 sheet of paper. So it has been very much an exercise in contraction as I have aimed at highlighting the underlying principles that drove these people and what results were produced. I have taken them in alphabetical order of surnames with the exception of the first, St. David.

Clearly my list is subjective and there are many more who are worthy of inclusion. This may come at a later date. At the moment daily readings for a month will have to suffice. I realise the choice of people covers a wide spectrum of church life from Anglican to Nonconformist, from Calvinist to Pentecostal, including Brethren and Independent Evangelicals. My bias might be noted for I have included a number associated with my home area of Maesteg as well as from my own ecclesiastical background which has been the focus of my service for the Lord. However, there are people mentioned from many parts of Wales and from various other strands of evangelical Christianity. Both men and women are included and for many of the men their wives had significant influence and gave valuable support to their ministry.

Some were highly educated with degrees and doctorates, others had little in the way of formal education. There were itinerant preachers, while others largely confined their ministry to one locality. A number faced serious persecution and personal injury and even found themselves imprisoned for their work of Gospel presentation. Some lived into old age, while others died quite young. Yet each one can instruct and challenge us as we view their lives and their ministry for God.

The truth is that so often we have little or no appreciation of our Christian heritage. Many wonderful preachers, teachers, innovators and missionaries have been raised up by God to do a great work yet have become largely forgotten by later generations. It is worth reading biographies to become inspired by the past into making greater efforts in the present which has a knock-on effect into the future as we learn important lessons from great Christians of former generations. It is important not to forget or as the Psalmist put it, "That the generation to come might know them." (Psalm 78.6). "We need to see how God has worked in the past to understand our place in the divine continuum of His dealings with mankind." (N.C. Funston in *Choice Gleanings*)

History is therefore very important. Indeed the Christian faith is based upon events in history, namely the work of Christ on the cross and His resurrection. It is always worth refreshing our minds about God's work from the past. In fact a key aspect of the Christian life is to remember. This we do regularly through the communion or breaking of bread service when through the emblems of bread and wine the death of Jesus is recalled.

So history focuses our attention upon what God has done in the past and can enable us to develop a vision for the future. We do not dwell upon the past to the exclusion of issues that face us in the present but the past can give us the courage to trust the Lord to do a great work in the future and also that we might become the instruments in His hands to accomplish His purposes for our generation.

The reading list at the end is the source for much of the material. I also hope it will be an encouragement for some to turn to those books and delve at a deeper level into the lives of these Christians from the past as this short book can be nothing more than a taster of greater delights. May God be glorified and His people encouraged through the lives of these precious saints from previous generations.

My thanks to Lynne Evans and my wife, Alison, for taking a great deal of time and trouble to proof read the manuscript and eradicate some of the worst errors.

Paul Young

ST. DAVID

(520?-588?)

*"Do not get drunk on wine, which leads to
debauchery. Instead be filled with the Spirit."
(Ephesians 5.18)*

The patron saint of Wales, who is commemorated each year on 1st March, was a remarkable and committed Christian. We have only a few details about his life and a number of legends have built up around his memory. Yet he served God in an age when Christianity was reaching a zenith in the Principality of the Welsh nation. His influence is recognised as having been extensive both within the borders of Wales and into areas of England, Ireland, Scotland and Brittany. He is even said to have visited the city of Jerusalem. He was in the tradition of the Celtic Church which was independent of Canterbury until the 8th century.

David is thought to have been born in south-west Wales, possibly in the area of present day St. David's, but we do not know the precise date. He was educated in the age of monasticism and therefore attended the monastery at Hen Fynwy in Cardiganshire on the banks of the River Aeron. His tutor was the learned St. Paulinus and David himself developed into a powerful thinker and public communicator. He was fluent in Welsh and Latin and in his travels preached the Gospel effectively with good results.

His work was facilitated by the conditions of the time. The roads, built by the Romans, were still in good condition despite the decline of the Empire, which led to the removal of the Roman armies from Britain. Also there was internal peace in Wales at that time which greatly reduced the risk for travelling itinerant preachers. The impact of his work was very great and Wales experienced a sort of spiritual revival at that time which affected people from the highest born and most noble to the least and poorest in society.

David often worked in harmony with Teilo and between them they founded monasteries (including Glastonbury) and over one hundred churches are named after them. The burden of his message was to honour God, praise Christ and glorify the Holy Trinity. He was also self-disciplined and abstained from wine and meat. He and his fellow monks lived frugally and yet provided food and lodging for travellers as well as looking after the poor. Their work was hard as they cultivated the land and pulled the ploughs themselves. They also developed crafts such as bee-keeping and all belongings were held in common with no personal possessions.

His personal conviction and teaching against alcohol caused him to be known as 'David the Water drinker'. Yet possibly that contains a double meaning. He was one who only drank water as opposed to alcohol but who also drank spiritually from the water of life: namely the Bible and the person of Christ. We remember the account of Jesus talking with the Samaritan woman by the well, "*Jesus answered, 'Everyone who drinks this water will be thirsty again, but whoever drinks the water I give them will never thirst. Indeed, the water I give them will become in them a spring of water welling up to eternal life'.*" (John 4.13-14). Clearly David drank deeply from the well of God's Word and was nourished in his soul as a consequence.

He stood for Biblical truth and opposed the error of Pelagianism. Pelagius was a British monk who lived in Rome in the 5th century. He taught that people were not born with original sin and therefore did not have a bias towards evil. He believed and taught that people had power in themselves to follow the example of Christ. David stood for the truth as revealed in the Bible that we are all by nature sinners who cannot find righteousness through our own efforts. David was so eloquent in opposing the false teaching that his fellow monks elected him to be Primate for the region.

Rhygyfarch who wrote about David in the 11th century attributed a number of miracles to him. The most famous exploit was at Llanddewibrefi where the ground was said to have risen up so that David's message could be heard more clearly by the large crowd who had come to hear him speak. Obviously legends have built up around this wonderful man of God. In fact he is said to have advised Welsh soldiers in a battle with the Saxons to wear leeks on their hats to distinguish Welsh soldiers from their enemies. The result was that the leek become one of the emblems of Wales.

His name lives on in the cathedral of St. David's in southern Pembrokeshire which is built on the site of the monastery he founded. The area is extremely rural and so the presence of the cathedral makes the surrounding community the smallest city in Britain, hardly more than a village. David lived in the 6th century. "We do not know the year of his death (possibly it was 588), but we do know that March the first was the day." (Gwynfor Evans)

> *"There is a river whose streams make glad the city of God, the holy place where the most high dwells."*
> *(Psalm 46.4)*

THOMAS CHARLES

(1755-1814)

**"For the word of God is alive and active. Sharper
than any double-edged sword…"
(Hebrews 4.12)**

Thomas Charles, who is forever associated with the North Wales town of
Bala and was described as 'the Lord's gift to the North' (Daniel Rowland),
was actually born in South Wales. He hailed from Carmarthenshire, being
the son of Rees and Jael Charles, and was initially educated locally and
then at Jesus College, Oxford where he achieved a B.A. in 1779. At the
age of 17 he was converted under the ministry of Daniel Rowland and
during his time at university he met with a circle of evangelical friends.
For a time he also studied theology under the hymn-writing minister John
Newton of Olney.

Thomas was ordained into the Anglican church in 1778 and took up
curacies in a number of churches in Somerset. These he resigned in 1783
to move to Bala where he married Sarah Jones, a shop-keeper. Sarah is
described as "beautiful, intelligent, very godly and with a fairly well-lined
purse". She was determined to remain in Bala and so he had no choice, if
he wanted her as his wife, but to move to the town. Also, the income from
her business helped to support his work, as his Bible-based ministry was
unacceptable to the local Anglican parishes which led him increasingly
to associate with the Calvinistic Methodist movement. The Church of

England denied him employment but the Methodists were keen to have his services so he formally joined them in 1784.

When Thomas arrived in North Wales it was at a time of deep spiritual darkness and so he set about trying to bring to the people the light of the Gospel. Initially this was by teaching the poor children of Bala in his own home but gradually he organised and trained various people to go into the surrounding centres of population and develop schools. He also introduced, despite some opposition, Sunday Schools throughout North Wales. Wonderfully in October 1791 a revival took place in Bala. 'It began during the preaching of Thomas Charles one Sunday evening, and by ten o'clock that night there was nothing to be heard from one end of the town to the other but the cries and groans of the people in distress of soul.' (Brian H. Edwards)

The revival was remarkable because fifty years earlier, when Howell Harris had visited the town, he was almost killed by a mob who were utterly ferocious. Harris had experienced opposition many times before but this attack was unprecedented resulting in him being unable to face going back to the town for many years. So, clearly, revival can reach unlikely places and change unlikely people.

Thomas was deeply concerned about the lack of Christian reading material in the language of the people and set about remedying this situation. He issued his *Biblical Dictionary* (in Welsh) in four volumes. He wrote a Welsh catechism, and later a shorter catechism, also publishing one in English for the schools in Lady Huntingdon's Connection. He helped publish and edit a Welsh magazine called *Trysorfa Ysprydol* (Spiritual Treasury), and also produced a Welsh spelling-book and Rules for conduct of Sunday Schools. Much of his material continued to be used throughout the nineteenth century.

The Scriptures were utterly central to Thomas' life and work. He encouraged people to obtain, read and study the Word of God and he, himself, was totally yielded to its message. In 1800 an impoverished girl named Mary Jones turned up at his door, having walked 26 miles in order to buy a Welsh Bible. Her need was just the tip of an iceberg as people were crying out for the Word of God. This made a big impression on Thomas and he resolved to rectify the paucity of Bibles in the Welsh language. These Bibles needed to be plentiful and cheap as the need was great and the people were poor. The Society for the Promoting Christian Knowledge (SPCK) had provided some Bibles but there were still not enough.

Later Thomas attended a meeting in London of the Religious Tract Society, of which he was a member, and laid before them the need for Welsh Bibles. The plea was heard and the foundation was laid for the establishment of the British and Foreign Bible Society. One of its first tasks was to produce a suitable Welsh Bible, under the supervision of Thomas, to help meet the growing desire of Welsh people to read the Word of God for themselves.

The communion service at Thomas' church in Bala, held on the last Sunday of every month, attracted many people and the great preaching festivals each summer made Bala a centre for Methodism in North Wales. Thomas also developed an ordination process for Methodist ministers and travelled to Ireland to report on the state of Protestantism in that country. He was not only a man of great ability but was devoted to God and His Word. He died just three weeks before his wife and they were survived by their two sons. It is claimed that Thomas was one of the makers of modern Wales and a great grandson became the first Principal of Aberystwyth University College.

"…Jesus…said…Suffer the little children to come unto me, and forbid them not: for of such is the kingdom of God." (Mark 10.14)

JOHN CORY

(1828-1910)

"Abstain from all appearance of evil."
(1 Thessalonians 5.22)

John Cory was born in Bideford in Devon but lived his life (after the age of three) in Wales and became well known as a businessman and philanthropist. His father set up a successful business in Cardiff involving ship-brokering, then he began exporting coal firstly as an agent, then on his own account.

John and his brother Richard took over the firm in 1859 and developed it into a thriving company. Eventually they established 80 foreign coal depots to feed the steam fired ships of the empire and acquired coal mines in the Rhondda, Neath and Ogmore Valleys. They were also part of the consortium that developed the Barry railway system and docks.

Yet success in business and the recognition this brought did not cause John to lose his essential Christian convictions. He always maintained a high level of integrity and took civic duty very seriously. He became an alderman on the Glamorgan County Council, served as a member of the Cardiff School Board for 23 years and was also vice chairman of the Barry Dock and Railway Company. Today a bronze statue of him is to be found in Cathays Park in the City of Cardiff.

He was a family man married to Anna Maria Beynon and they had four children, a daughter and three sons and his church allegiance was to the Wesleyan Methodists. He served the cause of Christ in a variety of ways, largely through membership of committees and by giving generously as the following list of some of the most noteworthy organisations that benefitted from his generosity makes clear.

He was president of the British and Foreign Sailors Society.
He was trustee and guarantor of Wesleyan Methodist Churches.
He gifted Maendy Hall at Ton Pentre to the Salvation Army.
He made donations to the Band of Hope Union. This also reflected the fact that he was a teetotaller and supported the cause of temperance.
He made donations to Dr. Barnardo's Homes. Clearly he had a deep concern for the poor and destitute.
He made donations to Soldiers' and Sailors' Rests in many towns.
He donated the original YMCA building in Cardiff.
He gave £3,000 to the Police Institute for its construction and maintained an annual support for its upkeep.
He supported University College, Cardiff to the tune of £6,500.
He also gave generously to the Seamen's Hospital and to the Infirmary.

Each year he gave away nearly £50,000 and on his death he made bequests of nearly a quarter of a million pounds to charities such as the Salvation Army, Cardiff Infirmary, the Bible Society and Muller's Orphanage.

Yet he was more than just a source of funding. He gave out a number of prizes annually to pupils of Cardiff Schools who showed proficiency in Bible knowledge. He supported the evangelistic ministry of Moody and Sankey when they came to Cardiff for mission meetings. When the biography of Moody was published in 1900 John wrote to Seth Joshua, "Feeling anxious to bring before the ministers of Cardiff a copy of the official authorised life of the late Mr D.L. Moody, believing that it is calculated to promote the revival of spiritual life and of gospel endeavour, which we all feel to be so essential, I send for your acceptance a copy of this work, trust the perusal of same will be very much blessed - with every good wish, I am, Yours sincerely, John Cory". Clearly he was deeply concerned for God's work to prosper as he focused upon the Gospel and did much to help forward the work of evangelism.

This Gospel focus was also evidenced by the fact that he preached regularly at the Wesleyan Methodist Chapel, also conducted a Bible Class and supported a colporteur (travelling Bible seller). He never allowed any business in his company to be conducted on a Sunday and at his place of work he kept a special room, as a tract room, storing thousands of Gospel leaflets for distribution as required. Every day his business commenced with a time of prayer for all the partners and the heads of departments.

John had a highly credible testimony as a Christian business man and throughout his career he had an untarnished reputation. He seemed utterly unaffected by the honours and recognition which he received.

He died a few months after his wife, having caught a chill while attending her funeral. In his will he stipulated that his children, as a matter of honour and affection for their father, give to charities at least 10 per cent of their income from his legacies. No doubt this indicated the scale of his own giving as John certainly excelled in the grace of giving.

"…see that you excel in this grace of giving…"
(2 Corinthians 8.7)

WALTER CRADDOCK

(1606-1659)

"And I will very gladly spend and be spent for you; though the more abundantly I love you, the less I be loved." (2 Corinthians 12.15)

Walter Craddock, whose surname is also spelt as 'Cradock' or 'Cradoc', was a Welsh Anglican minister who became an itinerant evangelical preacher and was one of the founders of the first independent church in Wales in 1638. He was born near Llangwm, Monmouthshire and was almost certainly educated at the University of Oxford, undoubtedly with the view to entering the Anglican ministry. However, at that time he did not know God and had not experienced His grace, something which was not unusual for ministers in those days as many entered the ministry without a personal experience of salvation through Christ.

On leaving university he returned to Wales and having heard about the powerful preaching of Mr Wroth went and heard him speak. Wroth has been described as 'a zealous puritan minister' and 'a true minister of Christ'. The excellent ministry of Mr Wroth had a deep and lasting impact upon Walter and brought him to faith in Christ. From then on he wanted to preach the Gospel, which he did effectively, motivated by a deep concern for the salvation of his fellow men and women.

This led Walter to take up the curacy at Peterson-super-Ely in Glamorganshire and soon afterwards at St. Mary's, Cardiff where William Erbury was the minister. These two men served God faithfully and yet their ministry resulted in them being censured. They found themselves deprived of their living on the spurious basis of unorthodox preaching and refusing to read the Book of Sports, which had been issued by James I in 1618 to encourage games on the Sabbath provided divine service had been attended.

From there Walter moved to North Wales and undertook a fruitful ministry in Wrexham but yet again he was dismissed essentially for simply preaching the Gospel with too much conviction. From then on his ministry was not confined to one place and he has been termed the 'first itinerant preacher in Wales'. During this time he influenced many people including Vavasor Powell who came to true faith under his ministry. For many years these two servants of the Lord worked together, as fellow-labourers, in the ministry of the Gospel as they formed a very effective partnership.

It was in 1639 that Walter, together with Mr Wroth formed the first church according to an independent model. This was at Llanfaches. Yet he continued his widespread ministry and was willing to preach to any group of people who would form a congregation whether inside church buildings or in the open air. Sadly there are always enemies of the Gospel and the more zealous the Gospel preacher, the more intense the opposition becomes. His enemies named any person of deep piety or who showed deep conviction about the Gospel, 'Cradockims'. Anyone identified in such a way usually found it not so much an insult as a badge of honour with no real disgrace attached to it!

During the Civil War Walter was driven from Wales and made his way to London. He supported the leadership of Oliver Cromwell and in 1645 conducted services for captured Royalist Welshmen after the battle of Naseby, where he preached in Welsh. He was later appointed the regular preacher at the Barebones' Parliament, at St. Margaret's Westminster. This was a short lived Parliament set up for a few months in 1653 and was dissolved due to an inability to function properly. It was called 'Barebones' after one of its members, a leather worker named, 'Praise-God Barebones'!

Essentially Walter was independent in his views of church government but totally agreed with the important doctrines of the Christian faith. It was his conviction that the Bible was true and that the Gospel was the answer to the soul's deepest need and such truths gave him the zeal and authority to proclaim the message even in the face of criticism and enmity. He was a humble man, who held a low opinion of himself, but had a very high esteem for his Lord and Master, Jesus Christ. Humility is the very characteristic which the Lord delights to see in His servants. The humble servant is the one whom God can use to great effect in Gospel service.

Walter was instrumental in helping to arrange for the New Testament to be printed in Welsh in a suitable form for ordinary people to read. He was absolutely sure of the doctrine of justification by faith seeing clearly that no one could contribute anything to their salvation as it is entirely by God's grace accomplished through Christ's finished work on the cross. He proclaimed that message with great simplicity and to very good effect. It was not until a century and half after his death (in London) that his sermons, expositions and observations were collected and published as his 'Works'.

> **"Therefore being justified by faith, we have peace**
> **with God through our Lord Jesus Christ."**
> **(Romans 5.1)**

ANNIE DAVIES

(1887-1956?)

"Singing psalms and hymns and spiritual songs …"
(Ephesians 5.19)

Annie Davies was born to Richard and Hannah Davies in Pontycymmer in the Garw Valley along with brothers William and David and sister Maggie. Together with her older sister and a group of young ladies she ministered in song during the Welsh Revival of 1904. Her father had been unable to work for some time after an injury in a mining accident and so family life was difficult. Her mother made ends meet by taking in lodgers and running a small shop. Eventually Richard was able to resume work, though not heavy mining and became a lampman in a colliery in the Llynfi Valley, and so the family moved to Nantyffyllon, Maesteg. He had been a choirmaster when they briefly lived at Clydach and so music and singing was part of daily life for this family.

Clearly Annie was brought up in a Christian environment which centred on prayer, Bible reading and Chapel attendance as members of Zoar Congregational Chapel, Maesteg. "There were daily family prayers every night before bed: father read scripture and mother prayed: I will never forget the fervour with which she prayed…something of eternity came to me through those prayers." (David, her younger brother) This did not, however, preclude interest in more 'worldly' activities and Annie was well-trained in singing by such teachers as, Mr. H. Davies of Dowlais and

Madame Clara Novello from Cardiff. This training in the techniques of soprano singing served her well as she contributed her musical talent to the work of Revival. She was the singer most identified with worship during the Revival being known as 'The Nightingale of the Revival', becoming closely associated with the hymn, 'Dyma Gariad' ('Here is love').

The great turning point in her life came in November 1904 when she went by train to Pontycymmer to hear Evan Roberts preaching. Even though it took her two hours to get in due to the pressure of the crowd she managed to sit next to her sister Maggie. She wrote, "I did not enter the meeting in the right spirit, the consequence being that I felt very indifferent and full of curiosity. I continued so until nearly the end of the meeting, when, just before closing Mr Roberts asked all those who could stand up and say in their hearts that they loved Jesus above everything else to do so." Sadly, she and her sister did not get up and at the close she "felt very unhappy, conscience spoke very loudly to me, it told me that I had betrayed my Saviour… I felt God could never forgive my countless sins. I tried to sleep and forget all about it but found it impossible to do so."

Eventually she went to a second meeting when the preacher was Rev. David Hughes and she wrote, "there was a greater power working there, my soul was moved to its depths, my tears flowed freely." She was asked to sing something and "with an irresistible force I leapt from my seat and sang "Here is love vast as the ocean"…I could not finish it as I was sobbing too much, I could not refrain from weeping throughout the meeting." So at the age of 18 she gave her life fully to the Lord and knew for certain that she was saved.

Afterwards she met with Maggie and Miss S.A. Jones and they decided to consecrate their voices to the Lord. She informed Evan Roberts of her call from God to that work and from then on she travelled with him throughout most of the Revival, singing both in Welsh and English. She was also known to lead in prayer and give help in conducting missions. Evan Roberts drew particularly close to her family and would stay with them for some much needed rest when the strain of ministry left him exhausted. It was reported in the newspaper, "Mr Evan Roberts has passed another quiet day at Nantyffyllon, Maesteg, with Mr and Mrs Davies, the parents of Miss Maggie and Miss Annie Davies, the lady evangelists. The lady evangelists say he feels himself quite run down; he is very weak, and that he has a very poor appetite. He has come here for complete rest, and has not received callers."

Of all the singers Annie probably had the greatest impact as she sang many hymns but is mostly remembered for 'Here is love'. She was sensitive to the way the Holy Spirit was working in people's hearts and so she would break into song at just the right moment and it had the effect of lifting the meeting to another level. Many people found themselves deeply moved, even reduced to tears as this soprano sang with such beauty and sensitivity. Clearly she was an emotional person and quite often would break down while singing as the impact of the words touched her own heart in a powerful way.

Essentially Annie's (and Maggie's) public ministry only lasted for the few months of the Revival (1904-05). Later they became nurses but their lives seem to have been largely lived in obscurity following the great days of Revival. In 1954 the BBC interviewed Annie as part of the commemoration of the golden jubilee of the Revival and she told Aneirin Talfan Davies, "After the meeting Evan Roberts spoke to me saying, 'You must come with me.' I went with him, and I was with him all the time that he journeyed to and fro."

"Every day will I praise you…"
(Psalm145.2)

JOHN ELIAS

(1774-1841)

**"The entrance of your words gives light; it
gives understanding unto the simple."
(Psalm 119.130)**

John Elias was, first and foremost, a preacher of the Gospel and when he
preached it was with such power that someone described it "as talking fire
down from heaven". He was undoubtedly a gifted orator, being a born
speaker and was blessed with a fine intellect which combined with the
power of God was to make him the most popular preacher of his day. He
was born in Abererch near Pwllheli to Elias and Jane Jones but was largely
brought up by his grandfather.

At a very young age John possessed the rare ability to read both Welsh and
English and for a brief period attended school in Caernarvon. On Sundays
the usual pattern was to attend the Anglican Church in the morning and
then walk long distances in the afternoon to hear Methodist preachers. It
was near Caernarvon while staying with Griffiths Jones, a local preacher,
that he first conducted family prayers while Jones was away. Such was the
quality of his prayers that news spread into the surrounding district and
people were amazed that he could pray in public. Griffiths Jones himself,
said "his prayers made us all marvel greatly."

Later he became the first ordained minister in the Calvinistic Methodist Connexion. This took place on Christmas Day 1794 and he wrote, "A day to remember was that one day - Christmas Day in the year 1794 - when I was received as a member of the Monthly Meeting, and permission was given me to preach the Gospel of Christ. I was then only twenty years and six months old, and only one year and three months old as a professor of religion." The latter term means that he only truly knew Christ as Saviour shortly before becoming a preacher.

In 1799, soon after moving to Anglesey, he married Elizabeth Broadhead who kept a shop in Llanfechell. They were happily and lovingly married for 29 years and Elizabeth was in full sympathy with his ministry for God always giving him great support. They had four children but sadly two died in infancy. Following the death of Elizabeth he married a widow named Ann Bulkeley (nee Williams) who outlived him.

Some saw John as strong-willed to the point of inflexibility and so found it difficult to challenge or stand up to him. However, John was a man with very definite convictions because he trusted the Bible totally. Having a passion for proclaiming the Gospel he could move congregations by his oratory, which was inspired and anointed by the Holy Spirit. His was not a shallow message but one anchored in Calvinistic doctrine which, at times, controversially embraced limited atonement. His ministry, however, was widely appreciated and he was considered an outstanding preacher in Wales at that time.

John, with the benefit of his logical mind, helped to draw up the Confession of Faith for his denomination as well as the constitutional deed that incorporated chapel buildings as property of the Connexion. He was a strong advocate for temperance as drunkenness was such a scourge in many families at the time. In addition he also wanted to keep Sunday special and spoke out against desecration of the Sabbath. He lent his support to the Bible Society and gave encouragement to the London Missionary Society and then especially in later life pushed for better education for ministers and for education generally.

He published numerous works on theological themes as well as on Christian doctrine and was a regular contributor to the Calvinistic Methodist periodical *Y Drysorfda*. He penned his autobiography but this was not published until long after his death. Thus his influence was great and he was held in high esteem by many people. Unfortunately, this produced some opponents who dubbed him 'The Pope of Anglesey' or 'The Methodist Pope'. In many ways this was a back-handed compliment as it emphasised the authority with which he preached and the positive effect, under the hand of God, his preaching had upon his congregations.

He died in 1841 and was buried in Llanfaes Churchyard near Beaumaris. It is estimated that 10,000 people attended his funeral and someone wrote, "Today, June 15, was buried the greatest preacher in Wales, and perhaps, the greatest in the kingdom. May the Lord have mercy upon his church, and favour her again with such a minister as Elias was, like a flaming seraph in the pulpit." So his earthly remains went into the ground but his true self entered into the glory of his Saviour's presence. Today he may be largely forgotten in his homeland but his name is written in Heaven and many found the joy of salvation in the Lord Jesus through his preaching.

"A word fitly spoken is like apples of gold in pictures of silver."
(Proverbs 25.11)

CHRISTMAS EVANS

(1766-1838)

"...in humility value others above yourselves."
(Philippians 2.3)

His name derives from the fact that he was born on Christmas Day, the event taking place in a small cottage in the parish of Llandysul. His parents were Samuel and Joanna and he was their middle child and was not expected to live as he was so fragile at birth, but live he did! His father died when Christmas was young and a farming uncle offered to take him in as a farm hand, his wages being just his food and board and as a consequence he received little education and no Christian example, as his uncle was a drunkard.

While growing up he had a number of experiences which could easily have been fatal. On one occasion he was stabbed, on another he nearly drowned, once he fell from a high tree with a knife in his hand and at one time was nearly crushed while on a runaway horse. He seems to have been miraculously preserved for the great work he was to do later in life. The evidence is that he was born into poverty and lived his life without much of this world's goods. He had no airs or graces and was not interested in fashion or even new clothes and had no ambition to be materially prosperous. He was genuinely more concerned for the work of the Gospel than his own needs.

By the age of 17, when he left his uncle, he couldn't read or write but then came the great turning point in his life when he was converted to Christ under the ministry of the Rev David Davies. This stimulated him to buy a Bible and he began to learn, by candlelight, to read and write in Welsh. Later he would learn to read English and eventually mastered Hebrew, Latin and Greek. Sadly his former companions did not understand what had happened to him and one night beat him with sticks resulting in the loss of an eye.

Joining the Baptist cause he commenced preaching. He was unprepossessing in appearance but at a gathering in Llanelli he was the first preacher of the day. The occasion was essentially social and was in the open air. People were meeting up with family and friends and it was all very informal. Other preachers had declined to speak on such unpromising terms but when Christmas was asked he agreed. As he spoke his tone of authority caused chatter to cease as people began listening intently. They were spellbound by his eloquence and under intense fervour could be heard "Gogoniant! Gogoniant!" ('Glory! Glory!') When he sat down tears were streaming down many faces as people felt the impact of the Gospel. The 'one-eyed preacher' was destined to become one of the most popular heralds of truth in Wales.

He married Catherine Jones and travelled with her on horseback (on the same horse!) to Anglesey. There he served on a salary of £17 per annum in a very small, rundown manse. Yet the work was blessed as the ten preaching places became twenty and 600 converts were added to the churches. So influential was his work on the island that he was known as "the one-eyed man of Anglesey". His preaching was compelling as he had a vivid imagination which he used to great effect. He was a dramatic preacher and "his preaching method was, in essence, allegorical." (Peters) Indeed he was favourably compared with one of the greatest imaginative, allegorical Christian communicators, and became known as "The Bunyan of Wales." His work was anchored in prayer and he had absolute confidence in Christ.

His work in Anglesey became increasingly difficult as chapels were built, pastors appointed and Christmas was expected to raise funds to maintain and develop the ministry. He did this on preaching/fundraising tours of the Principality. Then came the terrible blow of his wife's death in 1823. He was about sixty years of age and a local woman of some financial means was suggested as a possible successor, but he eventually married Mary Jones his former housekeeper in Anglesey instead. She was 35, while he was 61. They were happily married for the final ten years of his life. After his death Spurgeon, out of respect for her husband's memory, secured a small widow's grant for her from the English Baptist Fund.

After his second marriage Christmas and his wife left Anglesey and he spent 2 years as pastor in Caerphilly. These were among the happiest times of his ministry and he saw 140 converts baptised and received into the church. From there he went on to spend four years as a minister in Cardiff which were difficult as he faced declining health, division in the church and the disgraced former minister a constant thorn in his side. Yet 80 new baptised converts were added to the church during his time there. He finished his days back in his beloved North Wales, though he still went on preaching tours and it was in Swansea that he preached his final sermon. He was 72 and on returning to the house where he was staying he reached the stairs and said, "That was my last sermon". It was a prophetic statement as he declined rapidly and died the following Friday. The group gathered around his bed heard him say "Good-bye. Drive on!". He was buried in Bethesda and mourned throughout Wales.

"For I am already being poured out like a drink offering, and the time of my departure is near."
(2 Timothy 4.6)

PETER LEONARD GOULD

GOULD

(1887-1973)

"… to work with your own hands, … that you may
walk properly toward those who are outside …"
(1 Thessalonians 4.11-12)

Peter Leonard Gould was affectionately known as PL and was born and grew up in Cardiff. His parents were Christians and therefore he learnt about the Gospel from a young age. However, he did not make a commitment to Christ until the year 1904 when Revival came to Wales. The event where he decided to follow the Saviour was a Torrey and Alexander mission in his home city. From that point onward he never looked back in terms of Christian commitment and was baptised by immersion the same year.

At that time he joined the Brethren assembly at Plassey Street Gospel Hall, Penarth and this was essentially where he undertook his church work for the rest of his life. However, he did spend two years helping in the work of Hebron assembly in Cogan, Penarth and later at Mackintosh Hall, Cardiff for three years. The Brethren were a dynamic group who had reacted in the early nineteenth century to the sterility of both the established church and much of non-conformity. It developed spontaneously in Britain, Ireland and surprisingly in British Guyana, South America. One of its early strongholds was in Plymouth, which led to the name 'Plymouth Brethren'.

Later the movement divided into two main branches - the Exclusive and the Open Brethren. The Exclusive Brethren were strongly connectional and very inward looking. Open Brethren were welcoming to all who loved and were committed to the Saviour. The Open have been powerfully mission-minded, investing both resources and personnel in overseas missionary work as well as heavy emphasis on evangelism in the U.K. To help facilitate support and prayerful interest in overseas mission 'Echoes of Service' was set up in 1872 and this organisation continues to the present time, now named, 'Echoes International'. It does not direct or control workers as they are considered accountable to their local commending church and answerable to God.

The Brethren have tended to call their local churches 'assemblies' and for any of their number involved in full-time Christian ministry there needs to be a clear call of the Lord which is recognised by the local church. Generally these workers have 'lived by faith' which means looking to the Lord for support, a principle developed by Anthony Norris Groves, who was known as the 'Father of Faith Missions'.

It was with the Open Brethren that PL devoted his spiritual energies, supported by his wife Elsie. Their marriage was based upon love and devotion and they had two sons. Primarily PL's work was secular and he completed a long apprenticeship in his father's iron and brass foundry and eventually became Managing Director, a position he held for 35 years (1920-1955). He also managed an arc welding company and in addition held several public positions, including chairman of a number of federations. His services in this area of his life were recognised in 1955 with an O.B.E.

Yet for all his involvement in industry he was also deeply committed to outreach and missionary work. He supported tent campaigns for the preaching of the Gospel as well as conferences in Cardiff for Bible teaching and missionary reports. He was a member and for some time chairman of the Western Counties and South Wales Evangelization Trust which held many assembly buildings in trust. He was a trustee of Muller Homes for children in Bristol, which was the great social and evangelistic work initiated by George Muller, also a member of the Open Brethren, in the nineteenth century.

Later PL was asked to become a director of Stewards Company Limited which had been set up as a holding company for missionary property around the globe. This was to help give stability as mission workers tended to come and go and it saved them the need of getting involved with on-going ownership. Today Stewards is the parent company of the John W. Laing Trust. Sir John Laing was another member of the Open Brethren. In his capacity as director of Stewards, PL travelled to many countries and gained first hand experience of conditions and needs on the field of service. He was able to give sound practical advice as well as minister the Word of God in many places.

In 1955 he was asked to join the board of Echoes of Service and during the years in which he served he was noted for giving clear and insightful advice. There was no pretension but simple, brief and to the point comments that helped move decisions forward and he was a very great blessing to the work of mission around the globe. Sadly he developed a dreadful spinal condition which he bore with fortitude, undergirded by faith. There seemed to be no remedy and he went through many tests and examinations. Eventually he underwent surgery and recovery was a long painful process with him having to learn to walk again. After eight years of being at the heart of Echoes he retired but maintained his connection as a consulting trustee until 1966. Sadly his wife predeceased him going to be with the Lord in 1970 and three years later PL passed into the presence of Christ whom he had served so faithfully.

"… preach the gospel …"
(Mark 16.15)

ANN GRIFFITHS

(1776-1805)

**"Who can find a virtuous woman? For her price is far above rubies."
(Proverbs 31.10)**

Ann's life was short because she died in childbirth at the age of 29 but through her hymn writing (in Welsh) she has been hailed as a great contributor to evangelical Christianity in Wales. Her longest poem was described as "one of the majestic songs in the religious poetry of Europe." (Saunders Lewis). At the enthronement of Rowan Williams as Archbishop of Canterbury one of the translations of her hymns was included in the programme. Indeed Rowan Williams himself had translated the hymn: Yr Arglwydd Iesu (The Lord Jesus). She is generally considered to be an important figure in Welsh Nonconformist circles.

She was born Ann Thomas in the village of Llanfihangel-yng-Ngwynfa, Montgomeryshire to John Evan Thomas, a tenant farmer and local church warden, and his wife, Jane. The family was completed with three daughters and two sons, Ann being the fourth child and the youngest sister. She grew up in an isolated farmhouse, Dolwar Fechan, which is set deep in the countryside amongst the trees and streams. In the light of her parents' faith she was brought up an Anglican and therefore attended the local church.

Her mother died when Ann was 18 and around that time she followed her brothers and became increasingly drawn to the Methodist movement. She had previously been very flippant about those attracted to the Gospel and mocked anyone she saw going to preaching services. Yet on her way to a festival at Llanfylin she was persuaded to attend a preaching service and went home immediately afterwards "in a storm of troubled thought and dark questioning" (Elvet Lewis). Eventually she found the message of the Gospel to be the answer to her deepest spiritual need and she "became a strong and shining influence in the quiet valley around her home." (Elvet Lewis)

It was during a sermon delivered by the Rev. Benjamin Jones of Pwllheli that she decided to join the Calvinistic Methodist movement. One of the elders in the Calvinistic Methodist church was Thomas Griffiths a farmer in Meifod. Following the death of her parents, Ann married Thomas in 1804 but she sadly died the following year and was buried in the local graveyard of the village where she was born.

Her first hymn was composed when returning from a service in which she had been richly blessed. As she walked she felt full of her own unworthiness and yet paradoxically full of the glory of Christ. In a narrow, quiet lane she knelt in prayer and as she communed with God 'the spirit of sacred song touched her soul' and by the time she reached home she had composed the first verse.

It was her close friend and confidante Ruth Hughes, together with her husband John who helped publish Ann's handful of stanzas in the Welsh language. Ruth had been a maid in Ann's farmhouse and therefore knew her well, but also knew her poems because Ann used to recite them to her and she treasured them in her memory. Later she helped her husband to write them up in his notebooks. The hymns were published in 1805 and the notebooks themselves were published in 1905.

"Here, at last, the original version of the hymns is to be found. They are characterised by a wealth of scriptural allusion, by deep religious and mystical feeling, and by bold metaphors. They are written, for the most part, in an anucrustic 8-7 metre - a form which has given considerable trouble to composers of hymn-tunes." (Rev. Gomer Morgan Roberts).

Ann's poems clearly and powerfully reflect her fervent evangelical Christian faith, and her incisive intellectual ability as well as her thorough knowledge of Scripture. She is considered the most prominent female hymn-writer in Welsh and her writings are regarded as one of the great highlights of Welsh literature. She wrote in Welsh and so all we can do here is give a flavour of her work through translation:

He is called the Rose of Sharon
white and blushing, featured fair;
He excels above ten thousand
earthly things that men count fair:
Friend of sinners,
He's the pilot on the sea.

Ann is described as the "most exciting of all the hymn-writers, apart from Pantycelyn himself." (Gwynfor Evans) Evans also goes on to describe her as "a mystic who was a great theologian as well as a fine poet. One is amazed at the power of her imagination.. her great hymns will continue to enrich the spiritual life of Wales as long as the language lives"

"I tell you the truth, wherever the gospel is preached throughout the world, what she has done will also be told, in memory of her."
(Mark 14.9)

DAVID T. GRIFFITHS
(1895-1962)

"All they asked was that we should continue to remember the poor, the very thing I had been eager to do all along."
(Galatians 2.10)

David gave himself sacrificially to the work of God as he helped meet the needs of displaced people in Eastern Europe after the Second World War. His heart was so moved by the plight of those desperate people that he denied himself food in order to help supply their needs. In this he was fully supported by his wife Sarah (known as Sally). Together they served God and their example is a powerful challenge to our comfortable living today.

David was born near Cross Hands in South Wales and grew up to be a dedicated Christian. When the First World War commenced he, like many others, volunteered but was turned down as he was engaged in vital work in the coal mines at that time. Later, in 1916, he was called up but by then he had had a change of heart and mind as he saw things differently having decided to be a conscientious objector. This led to imprisonment in Wormwood Scrubs but had a positive spin-off on the work he was later to do in East Poland and Czechoslovakia. Since 1860, the people in those areas had chosen the custom of imprisonment rather than fighting and so he could easily make a point of connection with them.

On release in 1918 he and Sally studied at the Porth Bible Institute run by R.B. Jones. There they completed ministry training, married in 1921 and moved to Eastern Europe under the auspices of the Russian Missionary Society. They worked closely with Stuart and Mercy Hine. Stuart's memory lingers on today through the wonderful hymn, "How Great Thou Art" which he translated into English. However both couples severed their connection with the Society and came under the umbrella of Echoes of Service as part of the Open Brethren.

David and Sally settled in Baranovichi in Poland which was a transport hub on the border with Russia. It was here that they encountered thousands of refugees who were victims of the 1920-21 famine. In order to help feed these people and provide them with clothes, David and Sally impoverished themselves by using what resources they had to procure the necessary items. The result was that many trusted Christ as Saviour and were still going on with the Lord over 40 years later.

They then moved 200 miles to Zdolbunov and started work with the Hines. It was a time of bad harvest and the two couples survived for six weeks on a diet of haricot beans. "It was an unpromising beginning to what was to prove a close and blessed partnership in the Lord's service." (Tatford)

In 1924, David and Sally moved to Radzivillov and converted an old brewery into a Gospel Hall. It was constantly packed with many hundreds having to be turned away each week. Within 18 months 45 were converted to Christ. Also, in the surrounding villages, many women were saved through the medical and personal work of Sally. A strong Sunday School was developed with a good number of young people being brought to faith in Christ.

1934 saw them moving again, this time to Czechoslovakia. They arrived in Uzhgorod, the capital of Carpathian Ruthenia. Here in the very heart of an Orthodox area the people were much less responsive to the Gospel but still they pressed on proclaiming the glad tidings of Jesus. They engaged in personal evangelism, preaching and Sunday school work. There were notable conversions such as the man who had served the local Archbishop for 35 years and another who for 25 years had searched for the truth and found it after hearing David proclaim the Gospel.

They were obliged in 1939 to return to the U.K. and remained there for the duration of World War II. It was not until 1948 that they were able to resume full-time service in Eastern Europe where they travelled widely and David even visited Russia. Much of their work was with displaced persons and this certainly consumed a great deal of their time, but it was a ministry of mercy and spiritual blessing. They also had a ministry of joy, expressed in singing.

David loved to sing and sang in a quartet which included Stuart Hine, singing in languages they had come to know and love and some of the songs were recorded for radio ministry with programmes in Polish and Russian. "On one occasion at the Polish frontier a customs officer wanted to know if the harp that David was carrying was for sale. To prove that it was his own David burst into song and the customs examination stopped as the strains of, 'I know that Jesus loves me' filled the customs hall." (Tatford)

David's earthly pilgrimage finished in 1962 and Sally outlived him by two years. They had both suffered a great deal of deprivation, but rejoiced greatly as they had served God together with total devotion.

"…singing and making melody in your heart to the Lord."
(Ephesians 5.19)

HOWELL HARRIS

(1714-1773)

**"…pray without ceasing…quench not the Spirit."
(1 Thessalonians 5.17/19)**

Howell Harris, considered one of Wales' greatest preachers, was born in Trefecca, near Talgarth, Breconshire on 23rd January 1714. At the age of 18 his father died and he entered a very dark period in his life. Later he said it was 'a time when he first broke out in the devil's service.' Yet he never stopped going to the local parish church in Talgarth but sadly, the vicar was more interested in fox-hunting and drinking than in preaching the Gospel.

The vicar, however, did hold regular services and on the Sunday before Easter in 1735 he tried to encourage people to attend the following Sunday and said, "You say that you are not fit to come to the Table. Well then, I say that you are not fit to pray, yea you are not fit to live and neither are you fit to die." God used those words in a mighty way as they seemed to cut into the heart of Howell causing him inner turmoil. Over the next few weeks he searched for peace and eventually, after an enormous struggle, found it in Jesus. In his diary he wrote, "I lost my burden. I went home leaping for joy. O blessed day. Would that I might remember it gratefully evermore."

Howell now had an aim in life, which was to tell others about his new-found Saviour and so he started preaching in the open air. He applied for the opportunity to become an Anglican minister but was turned down three times. Yet he had a deep urge to preach the Gospel but with church buildings closed to him he began by standing on his father's grave which was in Talgarth churchyard. The plot was owned by his family and so he could not be legally prevented from standing on it to preach. This set the course for his public ministry and he has been described as "A flaming evangelist who felt a compassion for souls and a sorrow for all people who were in sin." (Martyn Lloyd-Jones). Preaching was something that utterly consumed Harris and was not a part-time occupation or some kind of optional extra.

Thousands heard him preach, including one young man who was passing and stopped to listen. He was converted to Christ on the spot and went on to become the celebrated hymn writer, William Williams of Pantycelyn, who wrote 'Guide me O thou great Jehovah' as well as 900 other hymns. Harris preached all over Wales and in many parts of England. Sadly he often met fierce opposition. He was badly beaten by a mob in Bala and in Machynlleth he was fired on with a gun. In Hay-on-Wye both he and his companion William Saward were pelted with stones by the crowd, and William Saward died as a result of the attack.

Howell Harris is considered one of the greatest Welshmen of the eighteenth century. He was a close friend of John Wesley and George Whitefield and was a founder of Methodism in Wales which became known as Presbyterianism. He knew God in a deep way and was living proof of Daniel 11.32: "The people who know their God shall be strong and carry out great exploits." He is listed in the book 'Welsh Heroes' (published in 2004), though more importantly his name is listed in Heaven.

He was considered a shy man and could be awkward in social settings, but he had great personal integrity and there was a holiness about the way he conducted himself. This resulted from his deep relationship with God as prayer was a cornerstone of his devotional life. He once wrote, "Being in secret prayer, I felt my heart melting within me, like wax before the fire, with love for God my Saviour. I felt not only love and peace but also a longing to be dissolved and to be with Christ; and there was a cry in my inmost soul, with which I was totally unacquainted before." Certainly Howell Harris lived in the realm of the Holy Spirit more consistently than most people.

He died in 1773 and was buried inside the church at Talgarth near the communion table where he first found peace with God through Jesus Christ. It is said that more than 20,000 people attended his funeral.

His life was not only one of preaching to great crowds and seeing revival come to Wales but also one of developing new farming methods and inventing agricultural machinery. In addition, he founded a community in Trefecca with its own publishing house.

Today Trefecca is a conference centre dedicated to the memory of Howell Harris and there is also a plaque commemorating him in Talgarth Church. Yet more importantly he was a key figure in the eighteenth century revival that swept through the Principality of Wales, resulting in a society that was transformed and spiritually renewed. Churches saw attendance grow substantially as a result of so many people being saved and the Gospel became both a force for good and a focus of attention throughout the land.

"So from Jerusalem all the way around to Illyricum,
I have fully proclaimed the gospel of Christ."
(Romans 15.19)

FRANCES RIDLEY HAVERGAL

(1836-1879)

"As for God, his way is perfect…"
(Psalm 18.30)

Though Frances Ridley Havergal was born in England and died at the young age of 42 she made a significant contribution to Christian mission in Wales, where she lived for a brief period of time. As a gifted poet she left some wonderful hymns which have been a blessing to generations of Christian believers and was a prolific author writing for both adults and children.

She was born into an Anglican family in Worcester where her father, William, was a minister. She may well have inherited her ability from him as he was also a composer and writer. She was the youngest of six siblings being particularly close to her sister Maria. Frances was academically gifted beginning to read books designed for adults by the age of four!

Sadly her mother, Jane, became ill with cancer when Frances was eleven and she found it very hard to accept that God would take her mother. One day as Frances sat by her mother's bedside, Jane said, "Fanny, pray to God to prepare you for all he is preparing for you." She never forgot those words and even recalled them a few months before her own death. Jane died in July 1848 and, as her siblings were living away, Frances felt very isolated, her diary entries reflecting the intense loneliness she experienced at that time.

Her schooling was unconventional as she was so advanced. Eventually she could read literature in a wide variety of languages: English, German, French, Hebrew, Latin, Greek and Welsh. She did attend school in her teens at Belmont in London and it was there that she committed her life to Christ. She wrote, "I committed my soul to the Saviour, and earth and heaven seemed brighter from that moment." She spent some time in both Germany and Switzerland (for study) and also ventured to Ireland, again for study, as her brother lived there.

One of her best loved hymns is "Take my life and let it be consecrated Lord to thee." It was written on a five day visit to Areley House. Ten people were in the house at the time and she prayed that each one would be somehow blessed by the Lord, whether to salvation or joy restored. The Lord answered her prayer and on the last night the two daughters of the house were crying and having talked with Frances, trusted the Saviour, their previous distress being replaced by joy. She was too happy to sleep and spent the night in praise to God and in renewal of her own consecration. Poetic couplets formed in her mind and continued until the whole poem was complete, finishing with the line, 'Ever, only, all for Thee.'

Frances had a love for the Bible. At school in Germany she set about learning great sections of Scripture by heart. She must have had a very retentive memory because she was able to memorise all the Gospels, the Epistles, Revelation, the Psalms, Isaiah and some of the Minor Prophets. It was an incredible feat but she was not simply interested in head knowledge. She passionately believed what she had learned and tried to live out what the Bible said. Her deep knowledge of the Word of God was eventually put to good use being reflected in her writing and the hymns she penned. She was so musical, with a beautiful singing voice, that she was often asked to sing solos and in addition she had an ability to train choirs at the various churches where her father was minister.

Frances helped to care for the needy through developing the Flannel Petticoat Society which distributed clothes to the poor, she collected money for the Irish Society and supported the Church Missionary Society. She also engaged in Sunday School work and kept in touch with many of the girls even when she became too focused upon writing to keep up the Sunday School work.

It was soon after her mother's death that Frances spent some time in North Wales. Presumably the break, away from home, was designed to help her adjust to being semi-orphaned. She later increased her connections with the Principality and "learned the Welsh language, using her own Welsh Bible and Welsh Prayer Book." (Carol Purves). In 1878, having suffered a bout of typhoid in 1874 which left her in a fragile state of health, she and her sister Maria settled in Mumbles (to the west of Swansea). There she had her own home and worked hard at her writing. Her study overlooked the beautiful Caswell Bay where she could see as far as the Devon coastline. However, her health continued to deteriorate and the feverish attacks to which she was subject became increasingly frequent. Many visitors came to see her including Ira Sankey, Elizabeth Clay (from the Punjab) and Baroness Helga von Cramm who had illustrated some of her books. As she approached the end of her life she was told (in answer to her question) that she would probably die soon and her response was 'Beautiful, too good to be true' and 'splendid to be so near the gate of heaven'. She was translated to glory on 3rd June 1879. A plaque commemorating her life can be found in Paraclete Church, where she worshipped during the short time she lived in Mumbles.

"…Sing unto the LORD, for he that triumphed gloriously…"
(Exodus 15.21)

JOHN HEADING

(1924-1991)

"…we look for the Saviour, the Lord Jesus Christ."
(Philippians 3.20)

John Heading was born in Norwich and was brought up as an Anglican. He was confirmed, took communion, taught Sunday School and gave general help to the vicar; yet at that stage in his life he was not saved. He attended the City of Norwich School and had an aversion to games & sporting activities but thrived academically, with a particular gift for mathematics, a gift he developed into his professional life. He took School Certificate and then Higher Certificate in pure mathematics, applied mathematics, physics and chemistry and a year later he was awarded an Open Exhibition to study mathematics at St. Catharine's College, Cambridge. However this was 1943 and he had lived his later school years under the cloud of war.

John's conversion was remarkable for its straightforward simplicity. He had been impressed by the demeanour of a teacher whom he helped in arranging Laboratory apparatus. Later, that same teacher gave John a Gospel magazine and also took him to a Gospel meeting. At that stage it had no impact upon him but it was laying a groundwork for future faith. June 10th 1943 was a day of 'coincidences'. Firstly, John had to cycle to pick up a book he had ordered. Secondly, the school teacher's wife saw him and asked him to take a package to the railway station for her son who had forgotten it. At the station John could not find the son either on any of the trains or in the station area, so he returned the parcel to his teacher's wife who invited him to go to the summer house where her husband was resting as he recovered from illness. In the summerhouse, his teacher wanted to talk about the Gospel. He simply read some Bible verses, explained their personal application and John's mind was opened. He became a Christian on that never-to-be-forgotten day.

Soon his new-found faith was tried as he entered the army with the Signal Corps. He was posted to various European centres and was greatly helped during this time by meeting Christians who were used by God to strengthen his faith, increase his understanding of Scripture and gave him opportunities to share his faith. While in the forces he left the Anglican communion and joined the Open Brethren staying with them for the rest of his life.

After army service he went to Cambridge where he was an outstanding student and gained a range of degrees in mathematics: B.A., M.A., Ph.D. & Sc.D. Clearly he had a powerful intellect being very gifted in mathematics. He became a Lecturer in mathematics, then Reader at Southampton University and eventually Professor of Applied Mathematics and Head of Department at the University of Wales, Aberystwyth, a position he held for 22 years before retirement. His list of academic publications, both in book form and also articles, is impressive.

Throughout his career, John maintained a strong ministry for God through various avenues. He was always faithful to the local church to which he belonged. In the 'backwater' of Aberystwyth the Brethren church did not have its own building; yet every Sunday he was there to lead, to preach and to encourage. Even though he was often away for preaching on Saturday evenings at various Bible teaching conferences he was always back for the Sunday morning service. He refused all preaching engagements that would have kept him from that small Sunday gathering of just a few dozen people.

He was responsible for a great deal of Bible ministry. This included both preaching and conducting Bible studies. His knowledge of Scripture was extensive and he was rarely unable to cite a verse of Scripture along with its reference. Many of those consecutive Bible studies were written up as part of his extensive written ministry as writing became a key area of his Christian work. He edited *Precious Seed* magazine for over 25 years, contributed articles to other Christian magazines on both sides of the Atlantic and wrote commentaries on Chronicles, Daniel, Matthew, Mark, Luke, John, Acts, 1 & 2 Corinthians, Hebrews and Revelation. He also compiled *A Dictionary of New Testament Churches*.

He was also a great encouragement to Christian students who attended the Brethren church. He and Margaret had been married in 1951 and together with their two sons had a home which was constantly open for hospitality. He encouraged students to preach and so gave them opportunities to develop their gift. He also produced a bi-monthly tract for distribution in the area and again students were encouraged to write these tracts under his editorial supervision as he was a superb proof reader. His support for mission work revealed great generosity and helped forward the work of God in many places. At his funeral, which I was privileged to take, the neighbours (non church-goers, non-academics) insisted on organising the catering and spoke highly of both John and Margaret Heading. Evidently their Christian testimony had an impact upon many lives because their faith revealed genuine love.

"… sorrow not, even as others which have no hope."
(1 Thessalonians 4.13)

REES HOWELLS

(1879-1950)

**"But Jacob replied, "I will not let you go unless you bless me"."
(Genesis 32.26)**

Born in the small mining community of Brynamman, Rees Howells lived a life of partial obscurity, but his story was related by Norman Grubb in *Rees Howells Intercessor* and made him a household name amongst the worldwide community of evangelicals. He was part of a big family with three girls, eight boys and parents: Thomas and Margaret. Rees was their sixth child and so was right in the middle and with such a large family life was hard and yet there was real Christian love in the home as his parents were committed to the Lord.

At the age of twelve he left school and took up employment in the iron works and then the coal mine but after ten years he emigrated to America in search of a better standard of living. There, at the age of 23, he nearly lost his life through a bout of typhoid fever and it dawned upon his mind what it meant to die without faith in Jesus Christ. A converted Jew by the name of Maurice Reuben was the means of Rees finding Christ. Rees wrote of the experience, 'I was born into another world. I found myself in the kingdom of God, and the Creator became my Father.'

Rees returned to Wales where he encountered the Welsh Revival of 1904-05 and was deeply influenced by the work of God's Spirit. Later, in 1906, at the Llandrindod Wells convention he unconditionally surrendered his life to God and from then on he was utterly and completely dedicated to God and His service. This could also be said of his wife Elizabeth whom he married in 1910. They had one son named Samuel Rees Howells who would later become the Principal of Swansea Bible College.

In 1915 the couple sadly had to leave their son in Britain while they travelled to South Africa as missionaries with the South Africa General Mission. While there they travelled over 11,000 miles and visited 43 mission stations near the Mozambique border. It was a remarkable time as revival broke out in all the stations and many people were drawn to Christ as a result. Yet after only five years they followed the leading of the Holy Spirit and returned to Wales in 1920.

Back in Wales Rees came to understand the need for two aspects of ministry which would have significant spiritual blessing. The first was the need for a Bible College to train Christians to be more effective ministers of the Gospel. This had elements of controversy to it as there was already a Bible Institute being developed in the Rhondda under the leadership of R.B. Jones. There was a feeling that Rees should support that initiative and not start a new training centre. However, he went ahead and in 1924 founded a Bible College in Swansea. It did not go well at first as there were disgruntled feelings as well as division amongst staff and students and so it closed. It took a whole year to facilitate a new opening with a new beginning. The aim was to be an interdenominational college which would give a thorough training to students in Biblical theology and also encourage the practical expressions of living by faith. He was College Principal for the first 16 years and gave himself totally to the work, urging his students to give greater allegiance to the Lord Jesus.

The college was founded upon faith principles following the model of George Muller with needs being mentioned only to God in prayer. A number of properties were purchased and a thriving work was established which lasted many years. During the war years a relative of the Emperor of Ethiopia was a student and incredibly the Emperor himself, Haile Selassie I, visited the college and stayed for some weeks on the estate of Penllergaer which had been newly acquired by the college.

The second aspect of his ministry was much less public and largely unseen and it was the development of a ministry of prayer. This is why Norman Grubb entitled his book, *Rees Howells Intercessor*. Rees recognised the importance of interceding with God and so gave himself to this ministry and every day, often for many hours, he wrestled in prayer. His was a prayer life that flowed from his devotion to Jesus, described by some as 'like a furnace' because of his total dedication. His prayers were focused upon the needs which he himself faced each day, also the needs of his family and of the college and finally the nation and the events of the world.

Throughout the Second World War, Rees prayed earnestly and almost continuously for the nation. He gave himself to prayer for Ethiopia when the Italians invaded. He announced publicly that God would defeat Hitler and the evil of Nazi-ism. He spent much time in prayer for the allied landings at Anzio. He believed that obedience and intercession should go hand in hand and said, 'As the crucifixion of the self proceeds, intercession begins.' His life as a devoted intercessor continued with constant passion until the day he died in 1950.

> **"…as a prince you have struggled with God**
> **and with men and have overcome."**
> **(Genesis 32.28)**

SELWYN HUGHES

(1928-2006)

"Our God…is able to deliver us…"
(Daniel 3.17)

Selwyn Hughes who was described by a former Archbishop of Canterbury as "a giant in the faith" came from humble mining stock in the small village of Fochrhiw and there he spent the first few years of his life. At the age of five the family moved to Birmingham where Selwyn felt alienated. Yet, in some ways, it prepared him for being more adaptable when other moves came later in life.

At the age of ten the family returned to Fochrhiw and he attended Bargoed Grammar School. As he grew up he felt pulled to the 'pleasures of the world' such as gambling, smoking and dancing but his parents, sincere Christians who attended the local Pentecostal Church, prayed continually for his salvation. At that time he hated Sundays, with three services and many prohibitions! Yet on a Sunday in February 1944 he listened to the sermon which seemed to be nothing special but God touched Selwyn's heart. He wrote, "I sobbed out my repentance before God and took the forgiveness He offered me through Jesus Christ His Son. Joy flooded my soul as God forgave my sin." He was dramatically altered and the Bible became central to his life.

Selwyn was baptised and later appears to have entered into the fullness of the Holy Spirit where the fear of man was replaced with an ability to talk freely with people about the Lord. He became a preacher of the Gospel even while working in the coal mine and such was the impact of his ministry that he knew the call of God to full-time Christian service. He trained at the Assemblies of God college in Bristol, where he developed a disciplined routine for daily life and studying Scripture. Over the next eighteen years he held pastorates in Cornwall, Wales, Yorkshire, Essex and London, yet Selwyn was destined to have a much more global influence than simply local work with an individual church. He married Enid Osmond in 1951 and they had two sons. They were devoted to each other and gave themselves in full commitment to the Lord's work.

Selwyn travelled widely and was even offered a lucrative pastorate in the USA and spoke to large crowds in Korea, Jamaica, Singapore and India. He helped organise and preached at the London Revival Crusade which was a series of evangelistic events from 1963-68 which resulted in many people being transformed through conversion to Christ. Later following a disturbing incident in one of his pastorates he learned the importance of counselling and eventually founded the Crusade for World Revival (CWR) with its focus upon personal counselling and also publishing the hugely popular daily reading notes, *Every Day with Jesus.*

The incident happened when Selwyn was minister of a church in South Kirby, Yorkshire. An unkempt, distressed man entered the vestry one evening, Selwyn hardly knew what to say to him and so simply responded to the man's outpouring of troubles by saying, 'I will pray for you'. The next morning the man's body was found in the local canal. Selwyn was devastated and overwhelmed with grief. He said, "From that day to this, I have striven, by every means possible, to develop counselling skills and to address people at the point of need." This was reflected in courses that he organised and published material he produced. He absolutely believed the Bible to be the basis for helping people but was not afraid to use secular therapies, though not all of them, as he aimed to bring the counsellee from self-centredness to Christ-centredness.

It was said that Selwyn enjoyed the largest daily congregation of any British preacher. This was due to the publication of his daily reading notes which went into 120,000 homes in Britain, and were read in 126 countries. In addition to the normal notes, there were notes for children, volumes for reading the Bible in a year plus many other studies and books. Eventually the CWR was located at Waverley Abbey House near Farnham in Surrey, England, which also became a centre for counselling courses and training.

Selwyn experienced a terrible blow when his wife was diagnosed with cancer and after a long illness died in 1986. He felt the grief very deeply and yet he could write, "Over the years I have often given advice to those who have been bereaved; now I have had an opportunity to test that advice in my own life. And what is my conclusion? It works - oh, how it works!" As he grew older he realised that he had failings and weaknesses which sadly had affected his family life. However he had always striven to improve with the Lord's help and through his devotion to the Gospel he did an immense work for God.

His legacy lives on in the 50 books he published, his recorded messages and in the lives which were changed by his ministry. The University of Brunel awarded him a Doctorate of Divinity for his services to Christian education.

"All scripture is given by inspiration of God, and is profitable for doctrine, for reproof, for correction, for instruction in righteousness: That the man of God may be perfect, throughly furnished unto all good works."
(2 Timothy 3.16)

GEORGE JEFFREYS
(1889-1962)

"Then they came to Elim, where there were twelve springs and
seventy palm trees, and they camped there near the water."
(Exodus 15.27)

George came from Nantyffyllon, Maesteg in the Llynfi Valley. He had two
brothers and nine sisters and life for such a big family was grim in those
days. His father was a coal miner but died at the age of 47. A number of his
siblings also died young and were outlived by their mother Kezia. Poverty
and unemployment were the realities that George experienced as he grew
up. Siloh Chapel, which he attended, was Welsh speaking and it was there
that George was converted to Christ under the ministry Rev. W. Glasnant
Jones, during the 1904 Welsh Revival. Subsequently he could always point
to the seat in the chapel where he was converted.

He entered public service for God with the Independent Apostolic Church,
Maesteg and then took on a much wider ministry. Yet for some time it had
seemed that he would never be a preacher as he suffered from a debilitating
paralysis which seemed likely to prevent him ever entering the ministry.
By the grace of God he was healed and 'gloriously set free in this way,
he pursued an energetic, indeed exhausting, lifestyle of over forty years.'
(Peters)

George spoke to vast numbers and was a compelling minister of the Gospel. Someone said that he was one of only two men who could fill a particularly large chapel in Cardiff and one of only three who could fill the Albert Hall in London. As a result of one of his campaigns in Cardiff a church was formed and became known as the City Temple which today meets in a large and impressive building. He often worked quite closely with his more out-going brother Stephen, as when they shared some months of ministry in North America but their different personalities and gifts caused them to separate. Stephen was more impulsive and outspoken, while George was more organised and very able administratively.

George founded the Elim Four Square Gospel Church, a denomination which continues and thrives to this day. The Elim movement was named after the oasis where the Israelites stopped during the wilderness journey as mentioned in the book of Exodus. The Four Square stood for the four points that George emphasised: Salvation, Healing, Baptism and the Second Coming. It is said that in addition to many becoming Christians at his meetings, some were also healed and this became an emphasis of his ministry. Elim is very much in the Pentecostal tradition and yet interestingly there is no Elim church in George's home town of Maesteg.

The first Elim church was founded in Belfast in 1915 and from that beginning came the residential Bible College. He was the first principal and generally was known afterwards as 'Principal George Jeffreys'. He also started a correspondence school, a publishing office, a printing works, a foreign missionary branch and innumerable Sunday Schools. It has been estimated that over 10,000 people were converted to Christ under his ministry.

Sadly, and with much personal anguish, after leading the movement for 25 years George severed his connection with the work he had started because of 'the totalitarianism of the Movement's Church administration and formed the Bible Pattern Church Fellowship with an inaugural rally at Westminster Central Hall in 1941' (Richards). The new movement produced a periodical entitled, *Pattern* and its key church was Kensington Temple in London though today the movement has largely died out.

George's zeal for the Gospel remained totally undiminished throughout his life as he carried on his work as an itinerant preacher and travelled internationally in the cause of the Gospel.

He was a man who deeply loved the Word of God and saw Scripture as being the absolute and only authority for the Christian church. He was also a man of prayer who communed daily with God and demonstrated an unswerving faith in the Lord. One day when asked for advice from a fellow minister he answered, "It is not your great faith that counts, but your little faith in a great God."

George never married and is buried in Streatham Cemetery, London. Yet his memory lingers and as we think about his work and testimony it is a challenge to present day Christians to be passionate, organised and focused upon the proclamation of the Gospel to our own generation. Peters describes George as "Unpretentious in his demeanour, he was truly a man of God." He goes on to ask, "What about us?"

"Therefore go and make disciples of all nations, baptising them in the name of the Father and of the Son, and of the Holy Spirit, and teaching them to obey everything I have commanded you. And surely I am with you always, to the very end of the age." (Matthew 28.19-20)

STEPHEN JEFFREYS

(1876-1943)

**"Do the work of an evangelist, discharge
all the duties of your ministry."
(2 Timothy 4.5)**

Stephen Jeffreys (whose name must always be associated with his brother George) came from the coal mining village of Nantyffyllon, Maesteg in the Llynfi Valley. At the age of twelve he followed in his father's footsteps and went to work in the local colliery and also attended the Sunday School in Siloh, a Welsh speaking Chapel, playing in their flute band. His Christian involvement was essentially nominal at best and he showed no aptitude for Christian ministry. Yet he eventually became a powerful and influential preacher who was used by God to change lives in many countries as well as various parts of the United Kingdom.

It was during the 1904 Welsh Revival that Stephen was saved. The exact date was 17th November 1904 and the preacher was the Rev. W. Glasnant Jones. So at the age of 28 he came to know Jesus as his Lord and Saviour and from then on he had one overriding ambition which was to tell other people about Jesus. He was a man of energy, with robust physical health, that enabled him to cope with a heavy schedule of travelling and with the pressure of continually engaging in the work of preaching the Gospel. Yet above all he was driven by a burning love for Jesus.

Initially he continued to work in the mine and served as an active member of Siloh while engaging in open-air preaching on the streets of Maesteg. One evening a large crowd gathered to hear him preach and an elderly lady living nearby brought out a chair for him to stand on. As it got dark she then came out with a lamp and held it up so he could be seen as well as heard! He never lost that love for proclaiming good news to the lost.

Stephen conducted evangelistic campaigns in a number of countries including the USA, Canada, Australia, New Zealand and South Africa. With the help of an interpreter he was also able to preach in European settings such as France, Switzerland, Italy, Germany and Scandinavia. This was a remarkable testament to the work of God in his life because he had never undertaken any form of higher or further education yet he could proclaim to large crowds wherever he went. His preaching had a powerful immediacy and he was also capable of preaching both in English and Welsh. Many cities in the UK were visited for missions and thousands of people were converted to Christ through his ministry. On one notable occasion it is said that a whole football team was brought to salvation through his preaching.

Some people viewed Stephen's work in terms of revival. After one gathering at Aberaman near Aberdare an aged church leader said that he had "seen three revivals but this is the greatest of them all." Someone described Stephen "as the greatest evangelist of the twentieth century." "He was a man of energy and humility; whose sense of purpose and conviction in preaching the gospel remained steadfast for almost forty years. His whole thinking was governed by the teaching of the Bible, which he believed with a child-like simplicity." (Peters) Somehow he knew the anointing of the Holy Spirit upon his ministry and was pre-eminently an evangelist who preached with passion and fervour and saw multitudes moved to trust in Christ.

Stephen took prayer very seriously and realised that it was not simply a duty for all Christians to engage in but a vital necessity for maintaining communion with God. He recognised that prayer deepened his relationship with the Lord. Allied with prayer was his faith which was utterly unquenchable and that was clearly seen in the last years of his life when illness prevented him from travelling, and he was characterised by patience and contentment.

He was married to Elizabeth Lewis, a farmer's daughter, on Boxing Day 1898 and they were blessed with three daughters (though one died in infancy) and one son. The son Edward became an evangelist who was also wonderfully used by the Lord.

As he was nearing 60 years of age and seemingly still in good health he was struck down with painful, debilitating arthritis. He retired to Maesteg and lived a quiet life with a limited amount of preaching. He gave his last sermon just a few weeks before he died at the Elim Church in Pontarddulais. He had been lovingly cared for by his wife and daughter but when his wife died in January 1943 it was a devastating blow. He died at his daughter's home in Mumbles, near Swansea on 17th November exactly 39 years after he was saved. His funeral was held in Maesteg and the Chapel was packed with people from all over Britain in attendance. He was buried in Llangynwyd Churchyard and as the coffin was lowered the large crowd sang: "In the sweet by and by we shall meet on that beautiful shore." The glory of Heaven was his.

"I have fought the good fight, I have finished
the race, I have kept the faith."
(2 Timothy 4.7)

GLYNDWR JONES
(1914-1995)

"I can do all things through Christ which strengthens me."
(Philippians 4.13)

Glyndwr Jones was always known as 'Glyn'. He acquired a fine reputation as a Christian gentleman and became a well known pastor in the village of Caerau, Maesteg in the Llynfi Valley. Today his name is carved in stone! There are some stone pillars in the village and inscribed in the plasterwork are names of local worthies. Amongst the names of doctors and sports people is Glyn Jones because he had served the community with dedication, prayer and proclamation with a constancy and consistency which all could see.

On leaving school he commenced work at the local colliery and was married to Lena. They had a large family, many of whom still live in the area of the Llynfi Valley. He did not become a Christian until he was in his thirties but he could point to a place in the Mission Hall where he gave his life in full commitment to the Saviour. The Mission is an unusual building. It has an amazing marble (very large) plaque behind the pulpit with various verses but most prominently, "We preach Christ crucified.". Also the pews are tiered and move from the level floor below the pulpit and step upward to the back wall. The main doorway is to the side of the building so one enters into the congregational seating area. It was part way up on the left hand side amongst the tiers of seats that Glyn knelt and trusted Christ.

Glyn's commitment was nothing if not total as he never deviated, for the rest of his life, from a whole-hearted devotion to his Lord and Saviour. To cement that commitment he wanted the world to know he was a Christian and so put a Bible verse on a banner and walked with the banner held high as he went to collect his colliery pay the week after becoming a Christian. It is said that the people came out of their terraced houses to see him walk by and many scoffed and said that they would give him three weeks and he would be back where he started, that it was just a flash in the pan. His subsequent life revealed that such thoughts were groundless, he proved them wrong.

Life was not easy for the coal miner, bringing up a large family, who had to work hard for his income. Yet every Sunday he attended services in the Mission Hall and never missed the weeknight meetings and was particularly focused on the prayer meetings. He was a man of prayer who loved to commune with the Lord. Even in public praying he could forget himself, praying for a long time, and yet one knew that he was experiencing something precious with His Lord.

He met tragedy with a calmness which had to be seen to be believed. He was a 'rare jewel of Christian contentment'. Two of his children in separate circumstances died tragically and it broke his heart but on both occasions the following Sunday he made his way to the Mission to worship God. Once a lady saw him and said, "Mr Jones I am surprised that you are going to the Mission today!" His response was, "Where else should I be?" He had to meet with God, which reflected his deep commitment to Christ but he also found that those services at the Mission helped to assuage the anguish he felt in his heart due to his loss. He did not blame God and was never bitter showing no animosity towards the Saviour. He demonstrated a quiet fortitude and faithfulness towards the Lord.

Glyn never advanced academically, having left school at a young age. He constantly mispronounced words but his messages had an immediacy and impact because they were anchored in Holy Scripture and supported by constant prayer. For many years he ran the Sunday School and young people heard the Gospel from his lips. He engaged in preaching both in the Mission and other chapels in the area of mid South Wales. He never learnt to drive and so had to rely upon public transport to take up those preaching engagements. He was also called upon to conduct funerals on a regular basis in the area, with many people booking him well in advance!

He could be eccentric at times and might preach at a graveside for 2 minutes or 52 minutes - one never knew what to expect. If Glyn happened to see you in the congregation, as I know from personal experience, he might suddenly call you up to pray or to even give a message. With Glyn one had to expect the unexpected! This was also an endearing part of his character.

He and his brother Ron were for many years elders of the Mission Hall congregation and when Glyn retired from the colliery he was invited to take on the role of pastor which he fulfilled with genuine kindness and love for the congregation who attended. His funeral was a packed event, with the Mission Hall full both upstairs and downstairs, with loudspeakers placed outside so that those unable to get in could listen to the service. It was my privilege, for which I thank God, to have been part of his Sunday School as a youngster and then to be one of two preachers to take Glyn Jones' funeral.

**"I have learned, in whatsoever state I am,
there with to be content."
(Philippians 4.11)**

GRIFFITH JONES
(1684-1761)

**"But grow in grace and in the knowledge of
our Lord and Saviour Jesus Christ…"
(2 Peter 3.18)**

Griffith Jones grew up in an age when there was no compulsory education and the vast majority of the working population of Wales were illiterate. By the time of his death he had brought about a massive change and raised the level of literacy to previously unimaginable heights. He was born in Carmarthenshire to John Ap Gruffydd and Elinor John. Initially he was educated at the village school and then became a shepherd for a short while. However, he had set his sights on becoming a minister of the Gospel and was able to complete his education at Carmarthen Grammar School. Such schools catered for those who desired further education and could afford it with the medium being the English language.

Griffith applied for ordination but was initially turned down but eventually was ordained as a deacon and in 1708 as a priest. He held various curacies before his appointment in 1716 to the rectory of LLanddowror in Carmarthenshire and it is with this parish that his name has become associated. It was his brother in law, Sir John Phillips, a man of great influence and an MP who gave him the living. He also supported him in any issue which arose with the authorities and he was blessed with the support of a pious and charitable wife named Margaret who predeceased him by five years. Prior to Llanddowror he had been closely associated with the Society for the Promoting Christian Knowledge (SPCK) and was interviewed with the aim of becoming a missionary to India with the East Indian Mission. In hindsight it was undoubtedly for the best that he did not go in view of the great work he did in his homeland of Wales.

Griffith was an outstanding preacher and was willing to preach not only in church buildings but wherever he could find a congregation. He also held preaching services on any day of the week. This often brought him into conflict with ecclesiastical authorities but nothing seemed to deter this preacher of the Gospel. "They came in their thousands from every corner of South Wales to listen to this passionate preacher…He satisfied the spiritual hunger of a nation that was tired of laxity and purposelessness." (Gwynfor Evans). Many were saved through his ministry, including another man destined to be very influential in Wales, Daniel Rowland.

Yet Griffith was more than a preacher or a local pastor. He "was an educator and organiser of genius." (Gwynfor Evans). In 1731 he set about teaching the people to read in their own language of Welsh and to this end he started to set up schools known as circulating schools, which travelled or rotated throughout the country. Each would remain in one place for up to three months and then it would move on. Such schools were open to all ages and were usually held in the winter months when farm work was slack.

The main purpose was for ordinary people to learn to read and the schools were greeted with great enthusiasm, so much so that evening classes were also held for those who could not meet in the daytime due to their work commitments. Yet Griffith's ultimate aim was that more people would be able to read the Bible for themselves and also learn the church catechism. By 1737 there were 37 circulating schools and 2,400 pupils and by the year of his death (1761) there were 3,495 schools with well over 150,000 pupils, which accounted for nearly half the population of Wales at that time. He was transforming the nation by making its people literate.

Such an undertaking took a great deal of organising and in addition Griffith took responsibility for teacher training. Clearly he was a man who worked hard and gave to the nation a sound basis for understanding through the medium of reading. Many see him as instrumental in saving the Welsh language from possible extinction as he believed it should be preserved, yet his main aim was the salvation of souls and to that end his work was also very successful.

Some wealthy landowners supported him such as Madam Bevan, who continued the work of the schools after his death until 1779. Griffith also wrote about thirty books, pamphlets and theological treatises and through the success of his schools and writings attention was drawn to commencing similar schemes in other countries. Indeed within three years of his death, a report was made by a commissioner for Catherine II of Russia who would have been delighted if a similar system could have been introduced into her realm.

So Griffith Jones was instrumental in enabling his fellow countrymen to be both literate - able to read the Bible and knowledgable - able to understand the Bible. This is considered by many to be the chief basis for the great Methodist Revival which was to sweep Wales in the eighteenth century. He was faithful to his generation and the Lord richly blessed the nation.

"I have more understanding..."
(Psalm 119.99)

MARY JONES

(1784-1864)

"So shall I keep your law continually for ever and ever."
(Psalm 119.44)

The story of Mary Jones and her Bible is widely known and carries a deep vein of pathos because it involves sacrifice and commitment. Mary was born in Abergynolwyn, Dolgellau, at the foot of the awe-inspiring Cader Idris mountain. Her father was a weaver named Jacob and her mother was Mary. Life was hard and money was scarce for her family and those of her community. Also few, if any, of her relatives or neighbours were able to read or write. Yet her parents were committed Christians who attended the local Chapel and it seems that Mary always went with them and had a great and deep respect, even reverence, for the Bible as the Word of God. She loved to hear the minister read from the Bible and longed for the day when she could also do the same.

That day came after she had learnt to read under the tuition of Mr and Mrs Evans who held a school in their home under the patronage of Thomas Charles' circulating schools. One day Mary was allowed to read a passage of Scripture during the Sunday morning service much to the pleasure of her parents and that also gave her a thirst to continue reading the Bible and a determination to have a Bible of her own. She was able to maintain her reading of Scripture from the only Bible in the area which was located with a family living two miles from her home. She frequently visited their home and they allowed her time to read God's Word.

Yet she continually yearned for her own Bible but the cost was high and availability was very limited. So she saved what little money she was able to obtain by doing various chores and after six long years she had enough to purchase a new Welsh Bible.

People in those days rarely travelled far from their homes and the nearest place for Mary to obtain a Bible was Bala about 26 miles away, which seemed an enormous distance. There Thomas Charles was known to sell Bibles. She decided to walk the long distance over difficult terrain, for most of the way she walked barefoot to preserve her footwear, and it was with great joy and excitement that she eventually arrived at Bala and made her way to the home of Thomas Charles.

Sadly, he had run out of Bibles but on listening to her story he, according to some accounts, gave her his personal copy. Others suggest that he waited a couple of days for a new supply to arrive and was so moved by her sacrifice that he gave her three copies for the price of one. Today one of those copies is to be found in the British and Foreign Bible Society's Archives in Cambridge University Library and inside that copy it says, "Mary Jones is the True Owner of this Bible. Bought In the Year 1800..." Another copy is lodged in the National Library of Wales but the third has disappeared without trace. These Bibles were the 1799 edition of the Welsh Bible of which 10,000 were printed at Oxford for the Society for Promoting Christian Knowledge.

Mary returned home triumphantly clutching her precious Bibles. Later she married a weaver named Thomas Lewis and moved to Bryn-crug, near Tywyn. She died in Tywyn in 1864 and was buried at the graveyard of Bryn-crug Calvinistic Methodist Chapel. Yet her memory lives on and her influence is still felt.

Thomas Charles who had been so moved by her story used it as an illustration for the Religious Tract Society to highlight the need for the production of more Bibles. This eventually led to the formation of the

British and Foreign Bible Society which today functions under the name of The Bible Society and has a worldwide ministry of distributing millions of copies of the Scriptures. So her epic trip which for those days was both long and arduous for one so young, was certainly not in vain.

At the ruin of her cottage home there is a memorial obelisk and on it are words commemorating her walk which led to the formation of the Bible Society. The memorial was erected by the Sunday Schools of Merioneth. Many people have now trodden the 'Mary Jones Walk' and retraced the journey she took all those years ago. This was particularly significant in the year 2000 which marked the 200th anniversary of her epic walk. In Bala the Bible Society has opened an exhibition centre known as 'Mary Jones World'. Many individuals have visited and also school parties have arrived in large numbers. So the story of Mary Jones and her Bible is one that inspires generations to be equally devoted to the reading and study of God's inspired Word.

Her story has been told and retold many times and she is a sort of national icon in Wales and a significant figure in Welsh Nonconformism. Yet our focus must always be upon the Word of God, encouraging people to read, believe and obey its message so that the blessing of salvation may be received.

"…but I have not forgotten your law."
(Psalm 119.61)

RHYS BEVAN JONES
(1869-1933)

"When the people heard this, they were cut to the heart..."
(Acts 2.37)

Rhys Bevan Jones was affectionately known as R.B. Jones and is closely linked with the work of God in the Rhondda. He was born in Dowlais to John and Mary, both committed Christians, and grew up attending Hebron Welsh Chapel located 200 yards from his home. He was educated at Dowlais Boys' School and later at Penydarren. Significantly, he gave his life to Christ at the age of twelve and knew from his early teens that he was called by God to be a preacher. His years of ministry were fruitful and richly blessed by the Lord.

Initially, Rhys worked in the colliery, then trained as a draughtsman but went on to an Academy at Aberavon for Ministry Training. There he attended Ebenezer Welsh Baptist Chapel, Cwmavon and met Lizzie Morgan, who would become his wife and they would have two children. He completed his training at Pontypool Baptist College where the focus was upon personal evangelism and the preaching of challenging sermons.

He was ordained at the age of 23 and took up his first pastorate at Berthlwyd Chapel, Treharris, where he honed his skills as a preacher. He wrote out his sermons in long hand and read them, though he was such a good speaker that it did not seem he was reading as he was expressive with an attractive voice delivery. It was at this Chapel that he became known as RB.

In 1895 Rhys became minister at Caersalem Welsh Chapel, Llanelli where he remained for five years. His ministry was described as 'unmixed success', with many being baptised and a number going on to become missionaries or chapel officials. By now he was considered 'the rising star of Welsh Baptism' (Brynmor Pierce Jones), was being invited to preach in many places throughout Wales and in 1899 he accepted a call to become Minister of Salem, a large and influential Chapel, in Porth. Salem had 400 members, along with 350 in the Sunday School and had planted two daughter Churches. All seemed well for fruitful ministry but sadly in 1901 Lizzie succumbed to illness and died at the age of 32. This profoundly affected RB and drove him to seek comfort through a deeper experience of God. Catherine Griffiths (Lizzie's cousin) came to look after the children and became RB's second wife in 1903 and was deeply involved in supporting his ministry.

At this time a number of ministers in the Rhondda were praying for revival and RB established a prayer meeting at Salem to seek God for a fresh anointing and soon 32 conversions were seen. Yet he hungered for a deeper work of God in his life and the 'Keswick in Wales' Convention under the ministry of F.B. Meyer was to prove significant. At that point RB gave up smoking, which was socially acceptable in those days, but more importantly he was personally transformed 'as a heavenly dawn broke over the souls of some of us.' From then on his preaching seemed to be revitalised and he had new energy with a desire to reach the lost becoming his top priority.

RB preached in many places and then accepted a call to minister at Ainon Welsh Chapel, Ynyshir. It was much smaller than Salem, with a correspondingly lower salary and was riven with division, yet he felt God was in the invitation. "The acceptance of the call to Ainon, was 'the most important single event in the life of RB Jones'. There is no doubt that he was walking by faith and not by sight." (Gibbard) Soon after that decision came the great moment in his life while conducting a mission at

Penuel Chapel, Rhosllanerchrugog (Rhos), Wrexham. There his preaching was described as 'a consuming fire' which brought deep conviction to the congregation. The Chapel was full each night, many were converted and revival fell on the local churches and the Lord's presence was felt throughout the area. This was the beginning of revival in North Wales and by the time RB returned to South Wales revival had broken out in Loughor under Evan Roberts.

Membership at Ainon went from 93 in 1903 to 195 by 1905, with 77 baptisms in 1905. RB continued to preach, especially in North Wales where he was seen as 'the Revivalist of the North' while Evan Roberts' work was largely confined to the South. In 1919 he accepted a call to Tabernacle English Chapel, Porth, where the church grew rapidly to 600 members with 1,000 in the congregation each Sunday. He did extensive preaching tours overseas to the USA, Canada and Latvia and also founded the Porth Bible Training School from which 40 students went on to serve in overseas mission and 14 in the home countries. Eventually the School moved and became Union Seminary now based in Bridgend.

The constant work broke his health and in 1933 he went to Egypt to recover, but sadly collapsed. He returned home and died on 15th April and was buried at Trealaw Cemetery. He was a man who loved his Bible, knew much of it by heart, and saw it as both pure and purifying. This fed his passion for preaching which reflected his deep devotion to Jesus Christ.

**"They devoted themselves to the apostles'
teaching…and to prayer."
(Acts 2.42)**

SAMUEL JONES

(1628-1697)

"To give…knowledge and discretion to the young."
(Proverbs 1.4)

Samuel Jones found his life caught up, challenged and changed by the interplay of political and religious movements in the seventeenth century. The decisions made far away in Parliament, London had a profound effect upon his life and ministry for God. The result was that he was removed from his living as a minister and became a very successful and highly regarded school teacher, with his own academy.

He was born in Chirk, Denbighshire, his father was John Roberts of Corwen and Samuel adapted his father's first name as his surname. We know next to nothing about his experience of growing up as a child but he was eventually well educated through spending time studying at All Souls College, Oxford and later became a Fellow and lecturer at Jesus College, Oxford. He took holy orders and was ordained in Taunton, Somerset and was later admitted to the living at Llangynwyd in May 1657. Llangynwyd was the original settlement in the Llynfi Valley and it has remained largely unchanged through the years right up to the present time. It is set on a hill and is dominated by the church, which is considered 'the mother church of the valley', there are also two public houses and a few private dwellings. The larger town of Maesteg has developed in the wide valley below.

Samuel Jones was made vicar of Llangynwyd towards the end of the Commonwealth Period, when Oliver Cromwell ruled the land, but it was not long before Charles II was established on the throne. This brought about the Act of Uniformity (1662) which resulted in what has been called 'The Great Ejection'. The Act insisted that the new Book of Common Prayer be prescribed for all churches and that all ministers had to be ordained by episcopal procedure. Over 2,000 clergymen refused to follow these instructions including Samuel Jones and so they left the established church and developed the concept of non-conformity.

Samuel refused to give unqualified acceptance to the 1662 Book of Common Prayer and also to being re-ordained even though it was thought that his ordination had not been conducted on strictly episcopalian principles but was rather more characterised by Presbyterian or Congregational ideas. This led to him being put out of his living at Llangynwyd. In some ways this was a great disappointment as he was a very good preacher but it seems to have worked out well and became a wonderful opportunity.

He set up a school in Brynllywarch, which was a farm further down the Llynfi Valley from Llangynwyd. Obviously in those days there were very few schools in Wales and universal education seemed out of the question. In teaching young people Samuel had found his God-given calling and was clearly extremely gifted for this work as he was very much a man of education and culture. He devoted his time to instructing and training young men for the ministry and his school, known as an Academy, was one of the first in Wales and developed such a high reputation, that it was called "The University of Nonconformist Prophets"! He was given assistance, through generous grants, from the non-conformist churches, especially the Presbyterian and Congregational fellowships. One of his students was Samuel Price who became assistant to Dr. Isaac Watts the great hymn-writer. Other students also achieved success and prominence following their education at Brynllywarch.

Samuel's gift as a communicator both of academic information and Biblical truth was widely appreciated and he was urged on a number of occasions to return to the Anglican community. However he was a convinced Nonconformist and remained true to his principles until the end of his life. He was considered a very tolerant man and under the Act of Indulgence (1672) was allowed to preach publicly. He secured several licences to preach and hold meetings as an Independent or Presbyterian, as to him there was little difference between the two.

This fine preacher, educational visionary, gifted teacher and opinion former died in July 1697 and was buried in Llangynwyd Churchyard. He was said to have been 'highly respected by the gentry and by common folk.' and he left a great legacy of highlighting the Gospel through preaching and the ministry of Scripture as well as enlightening the mind through teaching and educating young people. His was a remarkable life that had a lasting influence both upon church and community life.

"Let the wise listen and add to their learning, and let the discerning get guidance - for understanding proverbs and parables, the sayings and riddles of the wise. The fear of the Lord is the beginning of knowledge, but fools despise wisdom and instruction."
(Proverbs 1.5-7)

D. MARTYN LLOYD-JONES

(1899-1981)

"For therein is the righteousness of God revealed from faith
to faith: as it is written, The just shall live by faith."
(Romans 1.17)

Martyn Lloyd-Jones was destined to be one of the great evangelical influences upon the United Kingdom in the mid twentieth century. He was born in Cardiff but grew up in Llangeitho and always went to chapel. He was a bright, intelligent young man who passed the scholarship for Tregaron Grammar School but, sadly, the family experienced financial trouble and moved to London where his father took up employment.

Martyn trained as a doctor at St. Bartholomew's Hospital, London and became highly qualified being appointed chief clinical assistant to Sir Thomas Horder who was physician to the king. Martyn's future looked financially secure with success beckoning as a Harley Street doctor and in his personal life he was married to Bethan Philips, who was also medically trained and they were blessed with two daughters. However, during those years he became a committed Christian as opposed to simply a church-attender, and this was to lead to a fundamental change of direction for his future life.

At the age of 27 God called him to full-time Christian ministry and he took up the pastorate of Bethlehem Presbyterian Church in Aberafan, Port Talbot. It had originated as an outreach church with the Calvinistic Methodist Forward Movement and by the time Martyn arrived it was still in debt and was not clearly focused upon the Gospel. His ministry (1927-1938) was to change the church dramatically. The debt was cleared, many people were saved and the church became totally committed to the message of salvation. So great was the impact of his preaching that it was described as a revival.

The change of direction in his life was vindicated in the face of those who had thought him foolish or some kind of romantic. He had been clearly led by God, and though it seemed he had acted sacrificially to serve the Lord, he said, "I gave up nothing. I received everything. I count it the highest honour God can confer on any man to call him a herald of the Gospel."

His life in South Wales was not restricted to his local church as Martyn preached all over the Principality and crowds came to hear him preach in both Welsh and English. Sometimes he had a medical surgery in the morning, preached in Welsh in the afternoon and English in the evening. So many came to hear him preach that some, who could not get in, were known to break a window pane and gather outside to hear him. They had permission from the local minister and would pay for repairs afterwards! He also made extended preaching tours to the USA where his ministry was highly regarded.

He then moved from South Wales to London to take up ministry at Westminster Chapel from 1938-1968 and it was here that he emerged as one of the most influential evangelicals in Britain. He had outstanding pastoral abilities, a great gift for preaching and communicating the Gospel and was heavily involved in student circles giving strong support to University Christian Unions by demonstrating the logic of the Gospel and its clear relevance to the twentieth century. He was a supporter of the Evangelical Library, contributor to the Puritan Conferences and travelled extensively overseas for preaching.

Martyn has been termed "the last of the Calvinistic preachers" and his preaching was called, "Logic on fire". He saw preaching as anchored in Scripture and so should be understood as "Theology on fire". He longed to see revival and prayed on a daily basis for such an outpouring on our land.

While at Westminster Chapel, he saw the building restored after the damage of the War years. Also attendance grew and membership increased until he was preaching to hundreds, even thousands, every week. His Friday evening teaching sessions were also well attended. Such ministry had a big impact upon numerous lives including quite a few who entered into full-time work for God. His influence lives on in the lives of those who heard him preach, and also through his recorded messages and the books he wrote.

His books are of outstanding worth, being clear and logical, with the power of the Holy Spirit upon them and are much in demand around the globe. He wrote on the Psalms, Habakkuk, the Sermon on the Mount (Matthew 5-7), Philippians and 2 Peter, while his books on Romans and Ephesians are classics and should be on every preacher's shelves! He also published books on the Puritans, the subject of preaching and the issue of depression.

He never lost his love for Wales and constantly prayed that God would bring revival to the nation. He died on St. David's Day, 1981 and was buried at Newcastle Emlyn, where over 900 attended the service at Bethel Chapel. Later a memorial service was held in Westminster Chapel with over 2,500 in the congregation to say 'Good-bye' to a great servant of the Lord.

"I shall be satisfied, when I awake, with thy likeness."
(Psalm 17.15)

WILLIAM MORGAN

(1545-1604)

"So shall my word be that goes forth out of my mouth: it shall not return unto me void, but it shall accomplish that which I please, and it shall prosper whereto I sent it."
(Isaiah 55.11)

There is some debate about the exact date of William Morgan's birth and the precise location of his grave, though, it is somewhere in the grounds of St Asaph Cathedral. This is surprising as William Morgan was a bishop of the Anglican Church, a powerful intellectual and a renowned translator of the Bible and the Book of Common Prayer. Many people now consider him to have been pivotal in helping to ensure the survival of the Welsh language.

He was born in Penmachno, Betws-y-Coed, a remote place in the middle of the mountains of Snowdonia, North Wales, where his father was a tenant farmer. He studied at St. John's College, Cambridge where he obtained B.A. and M.A. degrees in philosophy, mathematics and Greek. He then, for seven years, undertook studies including the study of the Bible in Greek, Hebrew and Aramaic, also focusing his attention on the works of the Church Fathers and contemporary Protestant writers which led to him achieving both B.D. and D.D. degrees. There can be no doubt that William was an outstanding scholar.

He was ordained by the Bishop of Ely in 1568 and took up his first position in Llanbadarn Fawr, Aberystwyth. He moved on to Welshpool and then to Llanrhaeadr-ym-Mochnant in 1578. It was here that he undertook the serious business of Bible translation from the original languages into the language of the people, namely Welsh. His work was published in 1588 and was a new translation of the Old Testament as well as a revision of the New Testament, which had been translated by William Salesbury in 1567.

William was married twice and had one son named Evan who succeeded his father as vicar in LLanrhaeadr-ym-Mochant. William's first wife was Ellen Salesbury and they were married before he went to Cambridge. Later, following her death, he married Catherine who was daughter of George ap Richard ap John.

In 1595 William was appointed to the position of Bishop of Llandaff. During this time he revised his first translation of the Welsh Bible as there were a number of printing errors and also produced a Welsh translation of the Book of Common Prayer. In 1601 he became Bishop of St Asaph, a position he held for the last three years of his life.

Though largely forgotten today by the general public in Wales, William is held up as the person who single-handedly, through his translation, helped save the Welsh language from oblivion. His Bible "formed the foundation of Welsh literary prose until the 20th century, and gave Welsh a uniquely high status among the Celtic languages of Europe." "In this way the Welsh language was restored to its original splendour and identified with what was most important and dignified. It is impossible to measure the enormous influence of these factors on the character, the mind and the culture of the nation." (Gwynfor Evans) Though the Bible was revised in 1620 by Richard Parry, with the assistance of John Davies, it was still known as the 'William Morgan Bible'.

It is very doubtful that William set out to save the Welsh language from being lost, being more interested in the spiritual needs of the people of Wales. Certainly his translation of the Bible enabled people in churches week by week to hear the glorious message of the Gospel in their own tongue. "From Sunday to Sunday in churches of Wales the Word of God would be heard in the language which was spoken" in the land. This was his outstanding achievement enabling the people of Wales to understand church services which up to that time had been in Latin and though the services were becoming Anglicised, most people in Wales did not speak English.

The 'William Morgan Bible' is often compared favourably with the King James Version (Authorised Version) of the English Bible as both were powerfully influential upon their respective language communities. However the English Bible was the result of many scholars getting together and bringing out the best in each other in order to produce the translation. In the case of the Welsh Bible it was one man's dedicated work which produced a translation that had dignity and refinement. It was used as the basis for education when Griffiths Jones commenced the circulating schools in the eighteenth century. Probably the English translator who most correlates with William Morgan is William Tyndale, upon whose translation the King James Version is largely based.

As has already been said the grave of William Morgan is unknown and unmarked but there is a slate plaque, which commemorates his life, close to the gates of the parish church where he undertook his great work of translation. There is also a memorial to him in St John's College Chapel, Cambridge.

"…keep my words…"
(Proverbs 7.1)

STEPHEN OLFORD

(1918-2004)

**"I have been crucified with Christ; it is no longer
I who live, but Christ lives in me."
(Galatians 2.20)**

Stephen Frederick Olford was a man greatly used by God as a Gospel preacher, teacher of the Word, writer, counsellor, church leader, pastor to pastors and one who engaged the media to proclaim God's message. He is included here because he lived as a young man in Newport, South Wales and left a lasting impression on many people. Lives were changed in the Principality through his ministry and he is still remembered with great affection.

He was born to missionary parents at Kalene, Zambia, but grew up in nearby Angola. where his parents served God with the Open Brethren being listed with Echoes of Service. Stephen became a Christian at the age of seven and at 14 was baptised. His young days in Africa gave him experiences that focused his mind on the important, eternal work which he would be called to do. On one occasion he found a snake nestling in his boot, once he was stung by a scorpion, at another time a leopard leapt through the open window of his room while he was in bed, thankfully it picked up the pet dog and departed by the same route leaving Stephen unharmed. One day he was by himself in a marshy bog, was sinking fast and his desperate cries were answered by a man who 'happened' to be walking within earshot and rescued him. These experiences gave him a sense of the hand of God upon him.

Yet he came back to Britain at the age of seventeen, with no real desire to serve God, intending to study for an engineering qualification and seek a good lifestyle. However, a motorbike accident nearly sent him to an early grave as he suffered concussion, developed pneumonia (before antibiotics were available) and was given only two weeks to live, but he still battled with the Lord refusing to be truly committed to Christ. A letter from his Dad, who was still in Africa and knew nothing of the accident, arrived. In it was written, 'Only one life, twill soon be past, Only what's done for Christ will last.' This broke young Stephen and from then on he gave himself in full surrender to the Lord and to the work of proclaiming the message of the Gospel. His physical recovery seemed utterly miraculous as God spared his servant for a great work in the future.

He trained for the ministry and became a Scripture Reader to servicemen during the Second World War. By now the family had settled in Newport, South Wales and Stephen had started a Young People's Christian Fellowship in the town. It had a big impact and "many…went on to become distinguished servants of God in pulpit ministry at home and abroad." (Phillips). He was also traveling all over the U.K. to take missions and meetings but by the summer of 1946 he felt spiritually dry and so he cancelled all his meetings and took an attic room to pray, read and study. He came to "2 Corinthians 3, 6,17: 'The letter killeth, but the spirit giveth life…Now the Lord is that Spirit: and where the Spirit of the Lord is, there is liberty.' This can be understood, where the Spirit is Lord - that is, where He is given His true deity and sovereignty - there is liberty! And God set me free!" From then on his preaching seemed to take on new power and a clearer direction, developing into a worldwide ministry. That year he met with Billy Graham, spending some time with the evangelist going over what he had learnt about the Holy Spirit. Billy Graham went on to say that Stephen Olford was "the man who most influenced my ministry".

In 1948 he married Heather Brown and they forged a strong marriage and their two sons continue in Gospel ministry. By now Stephen's ministry was widely appreciated as he had spoken at the Keswick Convention and preached in the United States. He became the minister of Duke Street Baptist Church, Richmond, Surrey, (1953-59) but was allowed time for travel in order to minister in other places. He supported Billy Graham's Harringay Crusade and his church welcomed 100 converts from those meetings. He helped develop a visitation programme to every home in the borough of Richmond called 'Operation Andrew' and the church also began broadcasting "A Voice to Cheer" for shut-ins. Stephen was dynamic, innovative and blessed by the Lord and a new, larger building was undertaken for the growing congregation.

From 1959-1973 he was the minister of Calvary Baptist Church, New York City. There he introduced monthly half-nights of prayer, pioneered Christian television programming with 'Encounter' and his Sunday services were broadcast on radio. In 1963 he was voted one of the ten most effective preachers in the USA & Canada. By now he was in demand at large conventions in many parts of the world; he attended the inauguration of the US President, and published numerous books which continue to be greatly appreciated worldwide. In 1980 he launched the Institute for Biblical Preaching, while Luther Rice Seminary created the 'Stephen F. Olford Chair of Pastoral Ministries' in his honour. Stephen Olford's desire and aim in life was "to live and preach with one objective the pursuit of God."

"It pleased God, who separated me from my mother's womb, and called me by his grace, to reveal his Son in me, that I might preach him." (Galatians 1.15-16)

VAVASOR POWELL

(1617-1670)

"They arrested the apostles and put them in the common jail."
(Acts 5.18)

Vavasor Powell, who is largely forgotten these days, lived during the turbulent times of the English Civil War which brought about the end of the monarchy, the execution of Charles I and victory for the Parliamentary forces. Vavasor witnessed the setting up of the Commonwealth under Oliver Cromwell (1649-1660) and then the restoration of the monarchy on the death of Cromwell when Cromwell's son Richard failed to command authority. This led to the enthronement of Charles II. Sadly Vavasor spent much of his time in prison accused of various crimes but essentially it was for preaching the Gospel of Jesus Christ in a simple and straightforward manner.

He was born in Cnwclas (Knucklas), Radnorshire and was the son of Richard and his wife Penelope whose maiden name was Vavasor. The evidence indicates that he was educated at Jesus College, Oxford and returned to Wales to take up school teaching. It was at this time (1638-39) that he came to a clear understanding of the Gospel and personally trusted Christ as his Saviour. This was largely due to the influential ministry of Walter Craddock and also through the writings of Richard Sibbes.

76

Vavasor joined Craddock in an itinerant preaching ministry throughout Wales and it is said that, 'So great was the zeal and diligence of Mr V. Powell, that he often preached two or three times a day. It was seldom that he spent two days in any week during the course of the year, without preaching'. He sometimes travelled as much as 100 miles in a week, preaching wherever he found an opportunity and there were few churches throughout Wales in which he did not preach. In addition he often preached at fairs and markets, on mountains and in villages and God blessed his faithful work with many people trusting Christ through his ministry and backsliders being restored.

Yet Vavasor is said to have endured more persecution and imprisonment than any other preacher of his day. His first arrest seems to have been in 1640 when he was accused of 'disturbing the peace by preaching'. Later in Prestatyn he was accused of 'Inconformity' but found not guilty. He then moved to London and later for a short while was a vicar in Kent. Eventually he was granted a 'certificate of character' from the Westminster Assembly and returned to preach in Wales in 1649. His preaching was of such a powerful nature that in 1649 he preached before Thomas Foot, Lord Mayor of London and in 1650 he had the honour of preaching before the House of Commons. One can hardly imagine such opportunities today!

In his personal life he was married to a widow by the name of Joan Quarrel but sadly they had no children. After she died he married Katherine Gerard who outlived him.

In 1650 Parliament appointed a Commission for the better propagation and preaching of the Gospel in Wales and Vavasor acted as one of the principal advisers to this Commission. Such responsibility lasted for three years and brought about the removal of some of the more incompetent ministers. Alongside his main work as a preacher of the Gospel he was also an author who published eleven books on theological and Biblical themes and his poetic gifts enabled him to write a number of hymns.

In 1660 with the Restoration of the Monarchy Vavasor was arrested for preaching the Gospel and though quickly released, was again seized after a very short period of freedom. This time he was incarcerated for seven years, firstly in Fleet Prison, London and then in Southsea Castle. He was freed in 1667 and preached in London (at Blue Anchor Alley in March 1668) and revived his preaching in Wales, especially in Montgomeryshire and South Wales. However, after preaching at Merthyr Tydfil in October 1668 he was arrested for the final time. He was twice examined by the local authorities firstly in Cowbridge, then at Cardiff Town Hall and finally after a hearing at the Court of Common Pleas in London, he was committed to Fleet Prison where he died after a painful illness. He was only 53 and was buried in Bunhill Fields Cemetery, London. His grave is therefore found in the same cemetery as another great Puritan preacher who lived and was persecuted in the same era as Vavasor. Like him, he too was a writer, but one whose fame has lived on throughout the generations. His name is John Bunyan.

As we reflect upon Vavasor's life we see him as a Puritan who stood against the worst excess of Armenian doctrine. He also faced up to and spoke out against the political powers of the day. Yet surprisingly he has remained a relatively minor figure in British seventeenth-century Puritan history. "Vavasor Powell deserves better of historians than to be dismissed as a millenarian enthusiast. In many ways, Powell was the most striking personality amongst the Welsh Puritans." (R. Tudor Jones)

"But Peter and the other apostles answered and said:
"We ought to obey God rather than men".”
(Acts 5.29)

EVAN ROBERTS

(1878-1951)

**"If we confess our sins, He is faithful and just to forgive
our sins, and to cleanse us from all unrighteousness."
(1 John 1.9)**

Evan Roberts was one of 14 children and came from the village of Loughor,
west of Swansea. His parents were Henry and Hannah and by the age of
12, Evan had followed his father in working at the coal face. His initial
education was limited but later he attended school in Newcastle Emlyn,
Cardiganshire.

On 29th September 1904 he had a life-changing experience in a chapel
service at Blaenannarch which ended with the preacher, Seth Joshua,
offering up a prayer in which he said, "Bend us, O Lord!" Those words
had a profound impact upon the sensitive Evan and he knelt in prayer,
repeating in tears over and over "Bend me! Bend me! Bend me!" His
desire was that he would be moulded to the will of God. People came
to comfort him and wipe his face as he stayed in that posture for quite a
while. It was a mighty and memorable moment in the life of that young
man. Three things overwhelmed him. Firstly, the love of God seemed to
forcibly impinge upon his mind. Secondly, his own unworthiness humbled
him and powerfully affected him. Thirdly, he was consumed with a deep
burden for the salvation of lost souls.

This proved to be a crucial turning point in Evan's life which radically changed him and which subsequently he referred to as "Blaenannarch's great meeting".

Yet for many years he had been reading, talking and thinking about revival. It was constantly in his prayers and often the subject of his conversation. It is reported that one night he came into the school building in Newcastle Emlyn after time spent with God in the garden and his face shone to the point of actually glowing. His great friend Sydney Evans was taken aback but Evan said, "I have got wonderful news for you. I had a vision of all Wales being lifted up to Heaven. We are going to see the mightiest revival that Wales has ever known - the Holy Spirit is coming - we must be ready." The words sound almost breathlessly hysterical but they proved to be prophetic.

The Revival started in November 1904 and has been called, "the invasion of Wales by the Spirit through Evan Roberts" (James Alexander Stewart). Evan travelled up and down the Welsh industrial valleys conducting services and a great spiritual anointing was experienced. Thousands were saved and many backsliders restored. It is said that "the presence of God was felt everywhere", as the atmosphere was divinely charged.

Churches were revitalized and moved out of lethargic complacency to Gospel action, with many new members being added. Drunkenness and crime decreased and family life improved for many people. Bad language and swearing were greatly reduced and debts, even of long standing, were paid.

Though there were other preachers, Evan Roberts was at the heart of this movement and he adhered to four great principles. Firstly, the need to confess all known sin - past sins must be put away and cleansed in pursuit of true holiness. Secondly, the need to remove everything that is doubtful from one's life and to forgive everyone - no one must be excluded. Thirdly, the need to obey the prompting of the Holy Spirit - obedience must be instant, total and unquestioning. Fourthly, the need to make public confession of Christ as Saviour and to be open about one's allegiance to the the Lord.

During the months of Revival through the end of 1904 and into 1905, Evan Roberts was constantly traveling, taking services and counselling people. The meetings could be long, going on for hours, often late into the night. Before the Revival it was difficult to get people into the chapels; after the Revival it was difficult to get them out! Evan became exhausted and spent time recuperating with the Davies family in Nantyffyllon, Maesteg. Eventually he appears to have had a breakdown of some kind and went to live in Leicester in the home of Mr and Mrs Penn-Lewis where he became a recluse for a time, refusing to see anyone and as a result received a certain amount of severe criticism from some quarters.

It would seem that he was raised up by God for a short, specific ministry as a catalyst for the work of the Holy Spirit in Wales. The effect was felt around the world as many places experienced the sparks of revival at that time. Charlotte Chapel in Edinburgh was one such place, as was Assam in India, as well as Welsh congregations in America and revival influences traced back to Wales were felt in Madagascar, Mexico, Europe and even further afield.

Evan Roberts lived much of his later life in England, engaged in intercession and writing. He returned to Loughor for his father's funeral in 1928 and said a few words which were a blessing to those present. He settled in Cardiff and died in 1951, by then a largely forgotten man. He was buried in the family plot behind Moriah Chapel, Loughor (where the Revival commenced) and there is also a memorial column to commemorate his contribution to the Revival.

"But without faith it is impossible to please God…"
(Hebrews 11.6)

DANIEL ROWLAND

(1713-1790)

**"Not by might, nor by power, but by my
Spirit, says the Lord Almighty."
(Zechariah 4.6)**

This remarkable man, described as "one of the princes of the nation"
(Gwynfor Evans), never moved up the ecclesiastical hierarchy but
remained a curate throughout his ministerial life. He was, however, such
an outstanding and powerful preacher that crowds, in their thousands,
came from all over Wales to hear him proclaim the Gospel. So many
were challenged, convicted and converted through his preaching that a
great revival took place in the country. As a contemporary and at times
a colleague of Howell Harris, and together with William Williams they
helped, under the hand of God, to alter the spiritual and cultural outlook
of Wales.

He was born in Pantybeudy, Cardiganshire, his parents being Daniel and
Janet Rowland. He grew up in an ecclesiastical environment as his father
was a church minister holding the living at Nastcwnlle and Llangeitho.
Daniel seems to have been educated at Hereford Grammar School and was
ordained as a deacon in 1734, which was also the year he married Eleanor
Davies. His ordination to the priesthood came in 1735 when he became
curate to his brother at Llangeitho.

At that time, however, Daniel even though religious did not know the Lord as his personal Saviour. He was living a double life with each Sunday given to church in the morning and then for the rest of the day, alongside his parishioners, he indulged in all kinds of notorious behaviour, including drunkenness. His life was turned around through the ministry of Rev. Griffith Jones, founder of the circulating schools in Wales. Jones came to preach at Llanddewibrevi, just a few miles from Llangeitho and Daniel having heard he was a powerful preacher was persuaded to go and hear him. He went with an arrogant attitude and it showed in his manner as he stood during the service. Mr Jones noticed him and is said to have suspended his message to pray earnestly to God for the young man who stood before him. He cried out asking the Lord to use the young man to turn many from darkness to light. How wonderfully that prayer was answered!

Daniel left that service a changed man as he had become a true Christian and his ministry was transformed from merely religious to being centred upon the Gospel and initially he thundered against the evils of society. Gradually, he learnt to emphasise the grace of God and joined forces for some time with Howell Harris and they travelled far and wide to preach. Eventually Daniel did less travelling and his name will forever be linked with one place, Llangeitho.

When Daniel's brother died it was Daniel's son who took on the living at Llangeitho and so, for a time, he was curate to his own son. However, he built a meeting-house which was separate from the church and when later he was deprived of his curacy he preached in that little chapel. He was offered other livings, some quite lucrative, but chose to stay with the people at the chapel. Thousands flocked to hear him preach and especially on communion Sundays. "Rowland's communion services were heavenly, but (he) felt deeply the absolute priority and unique authority of preaching in the power of the Holy Spirit." (Brian Edwards) He published some small books and also wrote a number of hymns.

Referring to Daniel Rowland, Howell Harris and William Williams, Gwynfor Evans described them as men of "uncommon stature … the great revival would not have reached such revolutionary proportions but for them. It made the eighteenth century one of the greatest in the history of Wales."

Daniel died in October 1790 and was buried in Llangeitho. His long ministry had brought about the conversion of many people including over 100 men who subsequently became ministers themselves, including the famed Thomas Charles of Bala. Daniel Rowland was a man of God who was so steeped in Scripture that some claimed he had memorised the entire Bible. "Daniel Rowland was always reading and in the study" (Lloyd Jones), and he was a man of prayer who knew the anointing of the Holy Spirit.

As an example of his power in preaching and widespread influence we can mention a certain man who went fox-hunting on Sunday mornings and went to hear Daniel later in the day. His attitude was one of insolence as he stood on a seat but the message was so powerful that his outlook altered and he sat down with his head in his hands, weeping. He was described as, "a haughty scorner deeply humbled." That night the man invited Daniel to his home for a meal and an overnight stay and from then on his life was marked by a sincere faith in Christ, which manifested itself in a clear and powerful testimony of transforming grace. He was a new man and thanked God for Daniel Rowland the instrument through whom he had received salvation.

**"I have hidden your word in my heart that
I might not sin against you."
(Psalm119.11)**

ROBERT JERMAIN THOMAS

(1839-1866)

"…he that winneth souls is wise."
(Proverbs 11.30)

Robert Jermain Thomas is hardly recalled today in his home country of Wales, having been martyred at a young age on the other side of the world in Korea. His life is an example of total commitment to Christ through proclaiming the Gospel to people who had never heard the message and today the thriving churches and missionary zeal of Korean Christians is testimony to the legacy he left.

Robert was born in Rhayader, his father become a Nonconformist minister at Llanover near Abergavenny. Robert was converted as a teenager, becoming a member of the church at the age of 15 and very soon began to preach. He was an outstanding linguist, mastering a number of European languages and also studied medicine for 18 months. He spent five years studying at London University and then was ordained as a missionary with the London Missionary Society.

He and his wife, Caroline Godfrey, set out for the Far East and settled in Shanghai. Sadly, after four months, Caroline died of a miscarriage and under the terrible strain of such circumstances Robert resigned from the

Society and became a lecturer of English and Chinese in Peking. There he met some traders from the Hermit Kingdom, as Korea was then known, and found that Catholicism had taken root in the country with up to 50,000 converts but they were devoid of Scriptures and Robert volunteered to take Bibles into Korea. For this undertaking he became an agent of the National Bible Society of Scotland who paid his expenses.

In Korea he quickly picked up the language and travelled around in disguise and at great risk to distribute Bibles. The risk was one of execution if discovered by the authorities who were totally against foreigners and would only trade with China their next door neighbour. This first visit made Robert only the second known Protestant missionary to enter Korea, with Karl Gutzlaf of Germany being the first in 1832. Robert spent two and half months in the country distributing tracts and New Testaments in Chinese as at that time no Christian material was available in Korean and educated Koreans were able to read Chinese. After that first trip he returned to China.

Later he joined the American ship 'General Sherman' to sail up the river to Pyongyang (now the capital city of North Korea). Its crew were warned to leave as Korea wanted no foreign trade but the captain took exception to being ordered about in such a way. A firefight took place and a number of Koreans were killed. The ship eventually got stuck on a sand bank and the Koreans launched a fire boat that caused the destruction of the 'General Sherman'. The crew, including Thomas, had to leap into the water and make their way to land only to be met by an antagonistic mob.

Thomas is said to have reached the shore shouting "Jesus, Jesus" and handing out his last Bibles. He was executed and died a martyr at the age of 27. Yet the story does not end there, his influence continued to live on and today Christians in Korea deeply respect his name and memory as the one who brought the Gospel to their land.

Bibles were banned in Korea following the 'General Sherman' incident and many were destroyed. However, some were used as wallpaper enabling people to read the Scriptures simply by looking at those walls. Indeed

Robert's killer was so moved by the countenance of the man he had killed that he realized he had killed a good man. He kept one of the Bibles and wallpapered his own home with the pages. People came from all around to read the words of the Bible and eventually a church was established in that place, with the man's nephew becoming the pastor.

Robert's sacrifice was not forgotten and his last resting place, an island in the river, is known to Korean Christians as 'Mr Thomas's Resting Place'. The Thomas Memorial Association was formed and the Robert Thomas Memorial Church was built, being dedicated in 1932. In the cornerstone was inscribed "The blood of the martyr…' The churches grew in Korea and South Korea has become one of the greatest missionary sending country in the world. Sadly, the North Korean regime brutally suppressed Christianity and the Thomas Memorial Church was destroyed. Incredibly when they came to build Pyongyang University of Science and Technology, which is a Christian University linked with a University in China, the site chosen was the area where the Memorial Church had once stood. Robert may be largely forgotten in his home country, but he is fondly remembered in Korea and has joined the long list of saints who have laid down their lives for the sake of the Gospel.

**"Precious in the sight of the LORD is the death of his saints."
(Psalm 116.15)**

LEWIS HENRY TRANTER

(1881-1976)

***

"He must increase, but I must decrease."
(John 3.30)

Lewis Tranter lived a long and active life for the Lord and for over 70 years he served the cause of the Gospel in a full-time capacity. His work was essentially amongst the Open Brethren and he was instrumental in founding a number of local churches and had the joy of leading many needy souls to Christ. Yet he was a private man and shunned all kinds of publicity. He wanted the focus to be upon the Lord and not himself and so towards the end of his life he instructed his wife to destroy all the records he had kept and therefore very little in written form survives of his life and ministry.

He was born in Carmarthenshire near the town of Ammanford where his father was the local railway station master. He grew up as a fluent Welsh speaker and so later he was able to conduct his meetings in both Welsh and English. On leaving school, Lewis was apprenticed to an ironmonger in the Rhondda Valley but this did not last long and he moved to work in Swansea at a large department store in the town.

He grew up attending the local chapel, where he heard the Gospel on a regular basis and also attended a young men's prayer meeting each Sunday morning. Clearly he was religious, quite devotedly religious, but was not saved. The moment of truth came while working behind the drapery counter of the store. There was no one else present except Lewis and the Lord and so there was no one to explain the Gospel afresh to him or lead him in a prayer of commitment. Up to that point he had known the Gospel academically but now the truth had penetrated his heart as he encountered the living God.

The encounter took the form of a conversation with himself about whether he was going to Heaven or Hell. He knew he was a Hell-deserving sinner but remembered Matthew 11.28, "Come unto me all you that labour and are heavy-laden and I will give you rest.". In a darkened cellar corner in the store he knelt down and gave his life to the Lord. It was the change produced by God that transformed the young man, still under 20 years of age, and from then on his life was heading in a completely new direction.

Lewis sensed the Lord's calling to go to London, with two aims in mind, to secure a job and to serve the Lord amongst the down and outs of the city. Yet he did not even have enough money for the first night's lodging so he spent time in prayer for the Lord's supply. God answered his prayer and the next morning in the post was a gift of four pounds which was more than enough and so he went to the capital city. This was really the beginning of a life of faith where he learned to trust God to meet his daily needs.

In London he served the Lord faithfully but increasingly felt a burden for the spiritual needs of his family and neighbours back in Wales as he prayed for them. So he returned to Ammanford and his prayers were wonderfully answered as he saw both his parents and his three sisters come to faith in Christ and was also instrumental in bringing assurance of salvation to the local chapel minister and his wife. This was the beginning of a fruitful ministry of Gospel proclamation.

For the next 72 years Lewis faithfully followed the call to proclaim Jesus as Lord and Saviour. He used a horse-drawn Bible carriage for many years and also conducted tent missions. He rejoiced with the upsurge of Gospel interest during the revival of 1904-5 but also remained faithful to his calling during the later leaner years. He lived for a short while in Somerset in the 1920s but his heart was in Wales where he returned and spent the rest of his life.

The characteristics of this man of God can be summarised as follows. Firstly, he was a man who loved, read and obeyed his Bible. He had read the entire Bible fifty times between the years 1904 and 1951. His preaching was anchored in the Word of God. Secondly, he was a man of prayer. He always seemed to be completely at home in the Lord's presence. His constant refrain was "Prayer changes things" and he believed such truth passionately. Thirdly, he loved to encourage small groups of Christian believers in the industrial Welsh valleys. These were small assemblies many of which he had been instrumental in setting up. One example was the Gospel Hall at Hengoed. He had started the work there and the first meeting place was the stable belonging to the local doctor. Eventually a purpose-built hall was erected.

Finally we can say of Lewis that he was an engaging personal evangelist, with a very real ability to relate to people. As he travelled by rail or bus he was always able to converse the Gospel with fellow travellers and whenever he was out walking he was constantly distributed tracts. Clearly he had a great heart for the spiritual needs of people and believed passionately that everyone needed to hear the Gospel.

"For when I preach the gospel, I cannot boast, since I am compelled to preach. Woe is me if I do not preach the gospel!"
(1 Corinthians 9.16)

WILLIAM WILLIAMS
(1717-1791)

"…it is good to sing praises unto our God…"
(Psalm 147.1)

It has been written that the hymns of William Williams have "both stirred and soothed a whole nation for more than a hundred years…" (Elvet Lewis). This prolific hymn writer was born at Cefn-coed farm in the parish of Llanfair-ar-y-Bryn, Llandovery, Carmarthenshire. His parents, John and Dorothy, were Nonconformists, John being a deacon of an independent church which at times met in a cave at twilight due to the fear of persecution.

Sadly, John died in 1742 and Dorothy moved to a nearby farm named 'Pantycelyn' which means 'Holly Hollow'! From then on William's name has been associated with that farm as he is known as 'William Williams Pantycelyn' or simply 'Pantycelyn'.

We know little of William's early life growing up on the farm but he was educated locally by a neighbour Morgan Williams who was trained in English and Latin. He also went to the school in Llandovery which was sponsored by SPCK. In his late teens he left home for Llwynllwyd Academy near Hay-on-Wye, having in mind the idea of training for medical work and he spent three or four years there.

The great turning point in his life came in 1738 when he went to a Sunday morning service at the church in Talgarth. "The service was cold and spiritless, and left scarcely any impression whatever on the young man's mind." (Elvet Lewis). After the service, however, crowds were drawn to the graveyard where Howell Harris preached with power and Holy Spirit anointing. The message had a swift and dramatic effect upon William and he never forgot the debt he owed to Harris. William "came out of that historic churchyard with the light of eternity in his eyes." (Elvet Lewis).

Having been converted, he now wanted to serve the Lord and so applied, despite his Nonconformist background, for ordination as a deacon in the Anglican Church in 1740 and he was appointed as a curate. However, due to his links with the developing Methodist movement and his zeal to preach the Gospel outside places which were considered "properly consecrated" he was excluded from preaching in the Anglican communion. As a result, he felt called to conduct an itinerant ministry in which he travelled on average 3,000 miles a year all over Wales for the next 50 years. He is said to have partially supported his ministry by selling tea! He preached and composed hymns but also showed great aptitude as an organiser and administrator of the growing Calvinistic Methodist movement. In each place he gathered groups of converts together in 'seiadau' (informal testimony meetings) and he helped to maintain those groups of believers. Each new locality required a new 'seiat' and the workload and mental burden upon him must have been immense but it was his organising genius that drew the movement together.

He married Mary Francis in 1748, a very capable woman, who had helped in setting up the circulating schools in Wales. She was musically gifted and would sing William's new compositions and they were blessed with 8 children. The two boys grew up to be Gospel preachers while sadly one girl died in infancy. They lived with William's mother in Pantycelyn. Mary being an only child inherited a number of properties and land, which when parts were sold, helped maintain the family as William took no salary for his preaching and also helped to pay for the publishing of his many books including hymnals.

Today William is remembered as "The Sweet Singer of Wales" while Howell Harris described William as "a master of song". In the judgement of many he "is the greatest of all Welsh poets and that this is something of very real significance, because here you have such an outstanding natural poet now under the influence of the Holy Spirit writing these incomparable hymns." (Lloyd-Jones)

In all William wrote 900 hymns most of which were in Welsh, though some were in English; his most famous hymn being, "Guide me O thou great Jehovah". This hymn features in the Top 10 Songs of Praise on a regular basis and was sung by soldiers of the Welsh Regiments in the trenches of the First World War. It is also sung at Welsh rugby matches but how many of those singing actually realise that it is a testimony to the faithfulness of God?

William's hymns are anchored in Scripture and are a theological commentary. They bring encouragement to Christian believers and have proved to be a great stimulus to worship. He stressed that focus should not be on self but upon Jesus who alone should be exalted. Having dedicated his life to promoting the Gospel, William went to his heavenly reward in 1791. He was buried at the cemetery of St. Mary's Church, Llanfair-ar-y-bryn. A huge crowd attended his funeral and they had to prepare over 500 pounds of cake for the wake! The funeral was a fitting tribute to "the greatest hymnist of the Welsh language…the greatest poet of Wales in any age." (Gwynfor Evans)

"…I am ready to preach the Gospel…"
(Romans 1.15)

CONCLUDING
THOUGHTS

As I have reviewed briefly the lives of these Christians from the past common characteristics have been very much in evidence. The first is that each one had a genuine experience of conversion to Christ and knew with certainty that they were saved. Today this is sometimes called an 'evangelical conversion experience' but Biblically it is known as the 'new birth'. It is the regenerating work of God's Holy Spirit in the lives of those who have believed in Jesus Christ and which deals with the issues of sin and alienation from God through the work of Christ on the cross and by his resurrection. Therefore none of these people were sinless or perfect. They made mistakes, took wrong turns but each knew forgiveness through Jesus Christ and the concentration here has been upon the positives of their lives.

Also, they knew that they had been brought into a deep personal relationship with God as Father which resulted in a life of prayer. Such prayer was more than the formality of words and much more of a communion and encounter with God. These people 'enjoyed' prayer which led them into a close walk with God from which they derived power for ministry and were able to undertake successfully the responsibilities God had entrusted to them.

Another aspect was their total confidence in the Bible as the inspired Word of God. They anchored all they taught and preached in Holy Scripture.

They had absolute assurance that the Gospel was the only answer to the problem of sin which is mankind's disobedience, knowing that through the Gospel men and women could be saved from sin and its consequences and enjoy forgiveness and eternal life.

This knowledge made them passionate about proclaiming the Gospel and seeking to win men and women to Christ. Today some people often deride this as the 'zeal of the convert'. However, if a beggar finds a source for food then he can often feel a responsibility to introduce other beggars to that source. In the same way these men and women could not force anyone to believe, but they could proclaim that what the Lord had done for them in supplying their spiritual and eternal needs, He could do for others.

They were so often courageous people, having to face opposition, danger, difficulty, mockery and even having to stand against heresy. They faced up to such challenges with integrity and faith, standing for truth and at times paid an enormous price but they never gave up. Each one endured to the end, whether their life was long or short. They suffered with their Master down here on earth and now they share glory with the Lord in eternity. We view, with wonder, such powerful examples of godly living and we need to follow in their footsteps with full devotion to the Lord.

"To God be the glory, great things He has done"

BIBLIOGRAPHY

LAND OF MY FATHERS: 2,000 years of Welsh History by Gwynfor Evans (1974, John Penry Press)

In Pursuit of SAINT DAVID Patron Saint of Wales by Gerald Morgan (2017, Y Lolfa)

Wales After 1536 - A Guide by Donald Gregory (2009, Gwalch)

100 WELSH HEROES: All the stories and results from Wales' largest on-line poll by Culturenet Cymru (2004, Culturenet Cymru)

THE A-Z OF CURIOUS WALES by Mark Rees (2019, The History Press)

Welsh National Heroes by Alun Roberts (2002, Y Lolfa)

History of the Llynfi Valley by Brinley Richards (1982, D. Brown & Sons Ltd.)

Dewi Sant Saint David by Elin Meek (2001, Gomer)

Christmas Evans: The Life and Times of the One-Eyed Preacher of Wales by Tim Shenton (2001, The Evangelical Press)

MARY JONES AND HER BIBLE by Mary Carter (1949, The British and Foreign Bible Society)

GREAT REVIVALISTS: 1700 to the present day by John Peters (2008, CWR)

Revival: A People Saturated with God by Brian H. Edwards (1990, The Evangelical Press)

WALES: Land of beauty and blessing by John Aaron and Gwyn Davies (2015, Day One)

SWEET SINGERS of WALES by H. Elvet Lewis (1889, The Religious Tract Society)

THE BEDDGELERT REVIVAL by Eryl Davies (2004, Bryntirion Press)

Frances Ridley Havergal: The English hymn writer and poet by Carol Purves (2010, Day One)

CARRIERS OF THE FIRE: The Women of the Welsh Revival 1904/05 their impact then, their challenge now. by Karen Lowe (2004, Shedhead Productions)

The Challenge of Revival by Paul Young (2006, Fairmeadow Books)

A Pictorial History of REVIVAL: The Outbreak of the 1904 Welsh Awakening by Kevin Adams & Emyr Jones (2004, CWR)

R.B.JONES: Gospel Ministry in Turbulent Times by Noel Gibbard (2009, Bryntirion Press)

Rees Howells Intercessor: The Welsh Coal miner, a Prince with God by Norman Grubb (1973, Lutterworth Press)

D. MARTYN LLOYD-JONES: THE FIRST FORTY YEARS 1899-1939 by Iain H. Murray (1982, The Banner of Truth Trust)

D. MARTYN LLOYD-JONES: THE FIGHT OF FAITH 1939-1981 by Iain H. Murray (1990, The Banner of Truth Trust)

Martyn Lloyd-Jones: In the Footsteps of the distinguished Welsh Evangelist, pastor and theologian by Philip H. Eveson (2004, Day One)

JUST AS I AM: The Autobiography of Billy Graham (1997, Harper Collins)

ONLY ONE LIFE: The biography of Stephen F. Olford by John Phillips (1995, Loizeaux)

TURNING THE WORLD UPSIDE DOWN: A Centenary Publication of Echoes of Service (1972, Upperton Press)

THEY FINISHED THEIR COURSE: A Record of some Brethren who were called home in the 1970s by James Anderson (1980, John Ritchie Limited)

THAT THE WORLD MAY KNOW Volume 9 Red Glow Over Eastern Europe by Dr. Fredk. A. Tatford (1986, Echoes of Service)

SELWYN: Every Day with Jesus, A biography of Selwyn Hughes by John Peters (1990, CWR)

SEVEN LEADERS by Iain H. Murray (2017, Banner of Truth)

Heroes of the Faith Magazine (January - March 2018, New Life Publishing)

Printed in Great Britain
by Amazon

82092169R00068